CISTERCIAN FATHERS SERIES : NUMBER TWENTY-NINE

JOHN OF FORD

# SERMONS ON THE SONG OF SONGS, I

# JOHN of FORD

*Volume One*
(SERMONS 1–14)

*Translated by*
WENDY MARY BECKETT

*Introduction by*
HILARY COSTELLO
Monk of Mount Saint Bernard Abbey

CISTERCIAN FATHERS SERIES : NUMBER TWENTY-NINE

# SERMONS ON THE FINAL VERSES OF THE SONG OF SONGS

CISTERCIAN PUBLICATIONS: *Kalamazoo, Michigan 1977*

# CISTERCIAN FATHERS SERIES

This translation is based on the critical Latin edition of the sermons prepared
by Edmund Mikkers and Hilary Costello and published in the series CORPUS
CHRISTIANORUM, *Continuatio Mediaevalis* XVII & XVIII.

Latin title: *Ioannis de Forda, Super extremam partem
cantici canticorum sermones cxx.*

© Cistercian Publications, Inc. 1977
Kalamazoo, Michigan 49008

Ecclesiastical permission to publish this volume was received from
Bernard Flanagan, Bishop of Worcester, 17 March 1977

ISBN 0-87907-629-1

Library of Congress Catalogue Card Number 77-3697
LC Classification: BS 1485.J6413

Available in Great Britain and Europe through
A. R. Mowbray & Co Ltd
Osney Mead
Oxford OX2 0EG

*Book Design by Gale Akins*
*Typeset at Humble Hills Graphics; Kalamazoo, Michigan 49004*

*Printed in the United States of America*

# TABLE OF CONTENTS

# SERMONS ON THE SONG OF SONGS, I

## INTRODUCTION

# INTRODUCTION

## THE LIFE OF JOHN OF FORD[1]

W HEN IN 1191 JOHN OF FORD became abbot of the Cistercian monastery of Ford in Devon,[2] he was already a man of considerable literary accomplishment. His Life of Wulfric of Haselbury was written while he was still prior to this monastery.[3] There is good reason to believe that he completed this work in 1185, though it is likely that he began writing it much earlier and may have started collecting material for it as far back as 1166 when he was still quite a young man.[4] In any case it enjoyed a long period of popularity in the late Middle Ages and was quoted at length by Roger of Wendover and others. Its author is clearly a man with an eye for elegant Latin; he is likewise careful in the use of his sources, preferring to give the facts or stories he had personally learned from eye-witnesses of the events. And this care for his sources is certainly characteristic also of the author of the commentary on the Song of Songs.

Nothing is known with certainty about his early life. If he was a young man when the bishop of Bath, Robert of Lewes, died in 1161, then we must place his birth in the 1140s at the latest.[5] But this is conjecture rather than fact. So too are the alleged historical details given on scant evidence by later bibliographers, unless they knew traditions that are no longer extant. As he is sometimes called John of Devon, or Devonius,[6] however, it may

3

reasonably be assumed that he was born in Devon. As a young man he entered the monastery of Ford, founded in 1136 by the monks of Waverly, which was itself a daughter-house in Eleemosyna in the line of Cîteaux.[7] Ford was situated in a remote part of Devon, but was well known on account of several renowned writers. The most famous of these was Baldwin. Until he became a monk in 1169, he had been a cleric in the diocese of Exeter. He must have been an outstanding man, for he was abbot of Ford in 1175, bishop of Worcester in 1180, and finally he was promoted to the Primatial See of Canterbury in 1184.[8] His considerable written works were probably composed while he was at Ford. Some of them have subsequently been published in the Migne Patrology.[9]

This literary tradition was continued by Roger of Ford, one of Baldwin's disciples, who dedicated to him his *Versus de Beata Maria Virgine.* It is this Roger who testifies that another monk, Maurinus of Ford, wrote the Miracles of Blessed Mary. Both these writers were living while John was abbot.[10]

When Baldwin was abbot he took John as a travelling companion to the General Chapter at Cîteaux.[11] And so John was able to visit several monasteries of the Order in England and France. No doubt he made many valuable contacts. Some time between 1175 and 1180 abbot Baldwin chose John to be his claustral prior. A few years later, after 1185, John went to Bindon in Dorset where he had been chosen abbot. Finally, in 1191[12] he became abbot of Ford, holding this position until his death in 1214.

During the period of 1198–1213 there were several references in the statutes of the Cistercian General Chapter to the abbot of Ford. Meagre though the evidence is, it is not without interest to know something about the responsibilities placed on John by the General Chapter and to discover the matters with which he had to concern himself. The first direct reference to him comes in the year 1198 when he and the abbot of Furness were given a warning and a penance for not attending the Chapter. The formula of the penance occurs very frequently in the Statutes and it does not imply any special disgrace: 'The abbots of Ford and Furness . . . shall not enter the abbot's stall in choir and they shall fast on bread and water every Friday until they present themselves at Cîteaux'. The abbot of Fountains was deputed to declare this sentence to John.[13]

Apparently he took this warning to heart, for the following year a similar warning and penance was given to the abbot of Quarr on the Isle of Wight, and this time it was the abbot of Ford who had to declare the sentence.[14] John must therefore have attended this Chapter. In the same year permission was given to William de Brewer to found a monastery at Dunkeswell in Devon, and it was for the abbot of Ford to send a community and an abbot there.[15] In fact this monastery was not founded until 1201, when twelve monks from Ford were sent, one of whom, Gregory, was elected abbot.[16]

John was again at the General Chapter in 1201 when together with the abbot of Waverly he was charged with the commission of settling a dispute between Quarr Abbey and the Benedictine House of Lyra in Normandy.[17] It arose from the fact that at its foundation in 1132 Quarr Abbey had been granted lands from which Lyra had the right of tithes.[18] Once a dispute of this sort had started, as it was bound to, it tended to drag on for years. It was certainly not cleared up by John of Ford for it is still the subject of an acrimonious legal quarrel in 1289,[19] but it undoubtedly involved him in journeys that he might well have desired to have been spared.

It seems that he was also present at Cîteaux in the following year, 1202, as there are three statutes that affect him personally. He was commissioned to carry 'patent letters' to Hubert Walter, archbishop of Canterbury (1193–1205), concerning a fugitive monk, Rotolandus, who had been subprior of Aberconway.[20] Hubert Walter had proved a good friend to the Cistercians when the king, John, had demanded a carucage from the Order in 1200, and he had intervened to save it in this time of crisis. Aberconway Abbey occurs again in the following statute. The abbots of Llantarnam, Valle-Crucis and Aberconway were reported to be careless about saying Mass: 'they celebrate rarely and abstain from the altar.' The abbots of Ford and Combemere in Cheshire were deputed to visit these Welsh houses and make careful enquiries about the charges.[21] A more severe warning is given at the same General Chapter to two more abbots of Welsh houses: Strata-Florida in Cardigan and Abbey-Cwmhir in Radnor. Trouble appeared in the Welsh houses as far back as 1195, when the prohibition against beer-drinking had been put into force, causing the laybrothers to take violent action. There is no mention of beer in 1196 when the laybrothers of Strata-Florida rebelled, but we may safely assume that it had some part in their excesses.[22] At any rate, in 1202 John of Ford and the abbot of Combermere were given the difficult task of dealing with this situation and of imposing a penance on the two abbots concerned. The prior, cellarer and any other obstinate officials and laybrothers were to be sent away from their monastery until the General Chapter gave them permission to return.[23]

Three years elapse before there is another mention of the abbot of Ford. Then in 1205 he was directed with the abbots of Fountains and Buildwas to settle the quarrels between the abbots of Margam and Neath, both in Glamorganshire, and between the abbots of Neath and Strata-Florida.[24] Also in this year the abbot of Woburn asked permission to reduce the monastery at Medmenham in Buckinghamshire. Permission to found this house had been given in 1201, and three years later a colony of monks had been sent from Woburn without the consent of General Chapter.[25] Whatever the trouble might have been the abbot of Woburn is asking in 1205 for permission to recall the monks. The abbots of Ford, Boxley in Kent and Beaulieu were directed to go to Medmenham and make careful enquiries about the state of affairs.[26] Their decision may have been favourable but the monastery was not finally established until 1212, possibly because of the Interdict.[27]

The laybrothers at Margam must have been a troublesome band. Details of their violence were given in the Statutes of 1206 where the abbots of Fountains, Ford and Buildwas were commissioned to deal with them. They were accused of a conspiracy against their abbot, and against the cellarer, whom they threw off his horse. Armed with weapons they forced the abbot to flee fifteen miles, barricaded themselves in the dormitory and denied the monks their food. The ringleaders were ordered to go on foot to Clairvaux, and no more laybrothers were to be received into the monastery.[28] Probably this rebellion too was partly connected with the beer prohibition.[29]

Only two more references to the abbot of Ford occur during John's lifetime. A dispute between the York diocesan Chapter and the abbots of the diocese was committed to the investigation of the abbots of Ford and Beaulieu in 1210. They were prevented by the Interdict from attending this General Chapter, however, and so it was the abbot of Savigny who had to inform them about this commission.[30] This is apparently the only time that John of Ford was involved in a legal dispute among the northern houses of the Order. Finally, in 1213 the abbots of Waverly, Ford and Thame in Oxfordshire are to settle a quarrel between the abbots of Beaulieu and Stanley.[31] But as it is the abbots of Wardon, Woburn and Dore who are dealing with this affair in 1214 and 1215,[32] we must assume that complications had arisen. In any case, by this time John of Ford was dead.

The effect of the Interdict on the Cistercian Order and John of Ford in particular has been told several times in recent years.[33] The fact that John had been confessor to King John from 1204 until 1207 did not save either the Order or his own abbey from the king's disastrous exactions.[34] He had certainly acted as almsgiver for the king while he was his confessor, though there are records of gifts from the royal treasury to the monks of Ford even earlier than that.[35] After three years of frustrating chaplaincy he resigned this position and proposed Henry, abbot of Bindon, as a substitute. A detail about the king's character can be seen in his sad reflection: 'I resigned and put forward as a substitute my brother, the abbot of Bindon, who at first seemed to get somewhere, just as I had done, but with the progress of time he could do little or nothing.'[36]

As the king was in constant need of money he demanded financial help from the Cistercians on several occasions. Strictly speaking they were exempt from these levies and could only pay them with the express consent of the General Chapter. But it appears that some of the houses contributed in 1203 and 1204, for in the former case at least they came under the censure of the General Chapter for their pains.[37]

Worse was to befall them. The Interdict had been in force for almost two years when John of Ford wrote the forty-first sermon on the Song of Songs which he entitled, 'A Lamentation on the General Interdict.' Indeed it is this sermon that makes it possible to date the commentary with some accuracy. The sermon must have been written in 1210, since John sorrowfully affirms that 'the common people are now waiting hungry without any participation in the sacraments for almost two years.'[38] Since England and Wales were laid under Interdict on 23 March 1208,[39] he had felt the spiritual deprivation of

Mass and the sacraments very deeply, although by this time the Cistercians were celebrating Mass once a week. Earlier even this had been denied them. Yet he had the loyalty and the discernment to realize that Pope Innocent III was guided by the highest spiritual motives: 'There is no doubt that in this matter the Church is acting under the influence of the Spirit of the Spouse.' At the same time we see his deep concern for the spiritual good of the ordinary people.[40]

As if interdict were not enough, the crippling taxation or fine that King John imposed on the Cistercians later in the year practically ruined the Order in England. This tax was levied in order to pay for his campaign in Ireland. Once again the monks were in a difficult position, caught between the king's demands and the need for consent of the General Chapter. When the abbots met the king to explain their position, their appeal to this principle was hardly likely to pacify the king. It only incensed him. He knew all about the General Chapter and what he was likely to get from it. Probably one of the abbots, Alexander of Meaux, the ringleader of the hard-liners, provoked him even further. And so, when he returned from Ireland, he demanded a huge fine. He must have known that the fine to be paid by Ford alone, 750 marks, was enough to cripple the house. He gave the monks only eleven weeks to pay. When John of Ford himself, hoping that their previous friendship might stand him in good stead, appealed on behalf of the abbots against the time limit, the king helped them to make up their minds by imposing an extra fine of 100 marks for each day's delay in payment. Reading Sermon 76 one would not be fanciful to see John of Ford heartbroken and despondent as he is forced to give orders to sell everything of value that the monastery possessed: oxen, cattle, sheep, lands and clothing, books and church furnishings, including even the chalices. The monastery, he tells us, looked as if it had been hit by fire. Their more unscrupulous neighbors jumped in and got what they could at the cheapest price. John remarks wryly, but not without spiritual depth and conviction, that now they have been reduced to a state of poverty, they should start reconciling themselves to the true spirit of poverty, the poverty of their profession too long abandoned.[41]

Although King John made his submission to the Pope early in 1213,[42] it was not until April or May of the following year that the Pope instructed his legate Nicholas to lift the Interdict on England.[42] This did not come into effect fully until July.[43] But before that had been done, while the country was still under censure, John of Ford died on 21 April 1214.[44] No doubt this explains why he was buried without the ceremonies to which he was entitled[45] and we would expect to have been given to a great abbot, a holy man, a spiritual writer who has been too little known or honored even until our own day.

## THE PREACHER, THE WRITER AND HIS STYLE

It is very likely that these sermons were first preached in Chapter, then written down and polished up later. As abbot of Ford John would have had the duty of preaching to his monks at least on the most important liturgical feast days. Many abbots took the liturgy of the day as the theme of their sermons, but there was also a tradition of using these occasions as a chance for commenting on verses of the Song of Songs especially when these formed part of the day's liturgy.[46] This does not mean that we now have the sermon just as it was preached. Although there are many places where John seems to suggest that he is preaching, this is a typical literary device for giving a feeling of immediacy to the subject.[47] In any case he had used the same device in his Life of Wulfric of Haselbury, which was certainly a literary composition.[48]

On several occasions he refers to the sermon he had preached yesterday or to the promise he had made in yesterday's sermon,[49] giving the impression that the sermon is being taken down by one of the monks as it is being preached. Similarly he refers to the sermon he will give tomorrow (*cras* or *crastinus sermo*).[50] And sometimes he lends weight to this impression by a reference to his prolixity or to the weariness of his audience.[51] He suggests that they will be more ready to listen to the continuation of the commentary after an interval.[52] On the other hand there are also several places where he makes it clear that he is addressing a reader rather than a listener.[53] Or again he refers to himself as a writer using a pen and ink.[54] There is no need to labor this point. In the later Middle Ages the sermon was a literary *genre*,[55] and John of Ford obviously thought of these sermons as a sort of discourse on the Church and the spiritual life.[56]

As there is only one manuscript in existence we are unable to trace the revisions, if any, which John made to these sermons. We know in the case of St Bernard and to a much lesser extent in that of Guerric of Igny that there was some revision both during their lifetime and after their death. From the manuscript evidence one can trace fairly accurately the various stages of the recensions.[57] This is not possible with John of Ford. However, there is one place which strongly suggests that some revision was made. Some of the brethren of the monastery had been disturbed by the teaching in the eighth sermon that 'the Lord Jesus had inherited his innocence from his virgin mother.'[58] John had therefore thought it wise to explain his meaning at further length and to give the sources for his teaching. A note in the margin in a thirteenth century hand tells us that 'this passage was inserted into the schedula after the sermon had been edited in order to satisfy certain people troubled about this teaching.'[59]

John of Ford is invariably sensitive to the latin *cursus*
and rhetorical devices. His sentences are well constructed
without being fussy or obscure. Indeed this very sensi-
tivity to the latin idiom makes it all the more difficult to
render his thought into good English, so that one is forced
to take liberties with the text. His use of alliteration and
assonance, though frequent, is rarely obtrusive. We occasionally find a clause like this: ' . . . *sed quasi columba in
cauerna maceriae, terram omnem amplitudinem angustam
reputant et ruinosam . . .* '[60] But this is certainly acceptable provided it is not overdone. He is moderate too in his
recourse to word-play to emphasize some paradox or anti-
thesis. For example, in Sermon 6, wishing to bring out the
contrast between two different types of grace, he says:
'*Illud enim est adesse Deum per cooperantem gratiam,
istud inesse Deum per uirtutem inhabitantem.*' [61] Having
made the point he does not attempt to press it home
insistently. One could contrast this with Guerric of Igny's
style in his First Sermon for Christmas, where a whole
paragraph is full of antitheses.[62]

John's imagery and descriptions are usually drawn, so it
seems to me, from personal experience. We may expect
him to be familiar with the farming methods of his day,
with building techniques,[63] with the blacksmith striking
white-hot metal on his anvil,[64] with the vineyards and vin-
tagers of southern England and France.[65] But he also
seems to be talking from experience when he refers to the
goldsmith and the goldbeater working in precious metals,[66]
to judicial procedures in a court of law,[67] to the wood-
turner at his lathe,[68] to the harpist skilled at his musical
instrument,[69] or to the storm at sea such as he might have
experienced several times when he crossed the English
Channel on his journeys to the General Chapter.[70]

Two characteristics are remarkable in his writings: a
practical, down-to-earth experience of ordinary things
joined with the ability to describe them clearly and

succinctly, and a balanced and moderate judgment. This latter trait can be seen most clearly in the way he dealt with the king's demands during the Interdict. While he insisted on the rights of the Church over against the exactions of the king, he advised the abbots in England to bow to the king's will in this matter since it is better to safeguard spiritual values and the spiritual needs of souls rather than to insist too strongly on rights concerning temporal wealth and property. It was a compromise. It did not suit abbot Alexander and his party among the abbots; it would not have suited Thomas Becket. But it was characteristic of John of Ford that he could accept such a compromise, and perhaps it is in some way indicative of his very English temperament.

SOURCES

In one place John refers explicitly to Augustine, Gregory the Great, and Ambrose as the Fathers from whom he has drawn his teaching.[71] But there are many other places where he is clearly quoting these Fathers or is influenced by them. While he does not mention Jerome by name, his interpretations of hebrew words are unmistakably dependent on the *Liber de interpretatione nominum hebraicorum*[72] which was probably in the library at Ford. Likewise there are many explicit and implicit quotations from the Rule of St Benedict,[73] as one expects from a Cistercian abbot. Further study will be necessary before we can establish any dependence on Origen or the other early Fathers. In the case of the addition to the eighth sermon mentioned above he is careful to support his teaching by an appeal to the authority of St Anselm and Guerric of Igny.[74] Among the writers of the twelfth century he mentions Bernard of Clairvaux, Gilbert of Hoyland, and Richard of St Victor.[75] But there is no mention either of

William of St Thierry or Aelred of Rievaulx; nor, surprisingly, is there any reference to Baldwin of Ford, his own predecessor as abbot, his tutor and patron.

Among the classical writers he quotes Vergil, Terence, Sallust, Persius, Horace and Juvenal. On one occasion he uses a quotation from Aristotle, rare indeed at this time, but he is probably dependent for this on a later work.[76]

There can be no doubt that the chief source for John of Ford's thought, as for that of all the spiritual writers of the Middle Ages, was Scripture. He quotes all the books of the Old Testament except the prophecy of Nahum, and all the books of the New Testament except 2 and 3 John and Jude. He may quote Scripture rather less frequently than Bernard of Clairvaux or Guerric, but as I have counted over 1,100 references to the psalms alone in these sermons—and this is by no means an exhaustive search for references—there is no reason to underestimate him in this respect. A comparison between John of Ford and Guerric of Igny will help to bring out some of John's characteristics in his use of Scripture. Since Guerric quotes the Psalms approximately ten times in each sermon and John about nine times in each sermon, it will be seen that they are equally adept in their quotations. One must bear in mind of course that John's sermons are on average considerably longer than Guerric's. Taking the Psalms as our standard of reference we expect to find nearly twice as many quotations in John as in Guerric. This is confirmed by John's 406 quotations from Isaiah and 39 from Zachariah as compared with Guerric's 226 and 17 quotations from these prophets. John quotes Daniel 25 times as against Guerric's 8 times, which might not be very significant. But he does seem to have had a special affection for St John's Gospel which he quotes 370 times, considerably more than twice as often as Guerric's 150 quotations. And he also has a special interest in the first three chapters of Genesis which he quotes 85 times as

against Guerric's 12. On the other hand Guerric quotes
Malachy more frequently than John does (13 as against
6), and even if his total number of quotations from
2 Corinthians, 95 times, does not exceed John's 118
times, it is considerably more than half, and indicates
Guerric's special love for this book of the New Testament.

The most frequently quoted text in John's commentary (apart from the texts from the Song on which he
is commenting) is John 1, 14: 'And the Word became
flesh and dwelt among us, full of grace and truth', which
is quoted 24 times. Other important texts used frequently
are: Ps 44, 3 (16 times), and 2 Cor 3, 18 (13 times). These
are of course fundamental texts for the mystical writers.
So too is 1 Cor 6, 17: 'But he who is united to the Lord
becomes one spirit with him' (14 times). But whereas this
text is used so frequently by St Bernard, it is found only
three times in Guerric's sermons. Another text that has
been considered fundamental to Cistercian thought is
1 Jn 4, 10: 'God first loved us'. But in fact John only
employs this text 4 times, while Guerric does not use it
at all.

In his interpretation of Scripture John does not make
use of the words, *tropologia, anagogia.* But he certainly
knows the medieval division of the four senses of
Scripture. For him 'the words of Wisdom have many
meanings' according to the capacity of the reader, and this
is intended by the Holy Spirit as an occasion for understanding the text in various ways.[77] To understand John's
spiritual teaching we need to look first at his method of
approach to Scripture. He takes each verse of the text and
interprets it in a threefold manner: applying it to Christ,
to the Church, and then to the individual soul.[78] Typical
of this method is the development in Sermon 78. The
text, *Caput tuum ut Carmelus . . . ,* is very briefly looked
at for its literal meaning (11–14). Then the words are
given their allegorical meaning by applying them to Christ

himself as head of the Church (14–101). There follows an application of the text to the Church (102–158) concluding with the formula: *Haec autem in ecclesiae suae laudem a sponso dicta sint.* Finally the same text is applied to the individual soul (159–231) beginning with a clear formula to show that this 'moral' meaning is now being given to the text.[79] Usually a whole sermon is devoted to one or other application; often it is the Church that is dealt with in one sermon and then the individual soul in the next.[80] Sometimes the same method is extended over a series of sermons, e.g. Sermons 59–63. Occasionally the text is applied to Mary instead of to Christ in the first place, Sermon 70, and this is followed by an application first to the Church and then to the individual soul in a single sermon, 71. It seems that in the first twenty sermons John of Ford had not clearly thought out this method of approach so that in these sermons one verse of the Song is used for a whole series of sermons, namely 3–10, 11–13, and 16–19. Nevertheless even here a similar pattern can be discerned in so far as John reverses the order and deals with the Church as the Body of Christ in Sermon 3–6 and then with Christ as head in 8–10.

This method is essentially indebted to the three senses of Scripture: historical, allegorical and moral.[81] For the medieval writer the historical sense includes every attempt to find the literal meaning of the scriptural text. John of Ford has a certain respect for this sense, which he sometimes calls 'the Gospel story',[82] *historia uetus*[83] or simply 'the history'.[84] In other places he refers to this as the *facies sermonis.*[85] Almost invariably, when beginning to comment on a verse of the Song, John sets out some brief exposition of the historical sense. This is indeed the first meaning on which the others rest, or perhaps it should be called the outer covering—the surface of the text and therefore the superficial meaning.[86] In Sermon 5 much is made of the double meaning that can be given to the words *'in milibus'*. Similarly in Sermon 40 there is a discussion of the use of *'tecum'* instead of *'tibi'* in the text.

Interest in the literal meaning is somewhat perfunctory or even condescending. It is usually little more than a pretext for an allegorical interpretation.[87] Now the fundamental principle on which John's interpretation of the Song rests is that Christ is the Spouse and the Church is his Bride.[88] This is the allegorical sense by which we find the mystery of Christ and the Church foretold in the Old Testament.[89] The Song celebrates the marriage union between Christ and the Church. In one place John talks of the glory 'with which Christ has united this same Church of his to himself in the bond of marriage'.[90] It is a marriage that began when Christ united the Church to himself by dying on the cross, but which continues to the end of time; for as John says: 'This is the interpretation of the Bride's breasts if we understand the Bride to be the Church, either in its early days of faith when it was first wedded to Christ, or as it is wedded to him at the present time, or at the end of the world when it will be wedded to him with the remnant of Israel.'[91] Thus in the last phrase he subtly unites the eschatological or anagogical meaning with the allegorical.

But John's predominant intention was to deal with the 'moral' sense: that is to say, to apply the text to any soul whom Christ has deigned to call by the glorious name of 'bride of the Word'.[92] Frequently this change from the allegorical to the moral sense is made quite clear by some such phrase as: 'Now it is opportune to consider how this same text should be accommodated to the soul thirsting for God.'[93] But since he uses the same word *sponsa* for both the Church and the individual soul, a distinction must be made between the Bride of Christ, *sponsa Christi*, which is usually though not always used of the Church, and the bride of the Word, *sponsa Verbi*, an expression reserved for the person who has attained to or who is earnestly striving after contemplation and wisdom. The 'moral' sense finds its most perfect expression in the person who has become wedded to the Word in mystical union or marriage,[94] and so John of Ford devotes many passages to various aspects of this union.[95] But he is also concerned with those who have not yet arrived at this highest degree of the spiritual life, placing himself in the lower category.[96] These are the *'adolescentulae'* or humble souls who obediently follow the teaching of their pastors and try to keep God's law.[97] Finally, there is a special place for those who have the pastoral office in the Church, those who have the care of souls. Several of the final sermons are devoted exclusively to this category, which John seems to place higher in the scale of his values than contemplative souls.[98]

## BACKGROUND, AND PLACE IN TRADITION

John of Ford tells us that the idea of commenting on the Song came to him suddenly while he was 'burning with the desire of God's love' and anxious to know what to do about it.[99] Yet he did not undertake it without consider-able study. He was very conscious of the commentators who had preceded him—the elephants and giants, he humorously but reverently calls them—who had entered so deeply into the various meanings given by tradition to the Song. No doubt he was thinking principally of St Bernard whose footsteps he was explicitly following.[100] The saint's commentary, written between 1135 and 1153,[101] had arrived at chapter 3,1. Probably Bernard had no intention of pursuing the Song to the end. After his death Gilbert of Hoyland, abbot of Swineshead in Lincolnshire, took up the commentary where Bernard had left off and in forty-seven sermons had reached chapter 5, 9. In 1172 he too died, leaving the commentary still unfinished.[102] At this point John of Ford later took over and completed the commentary in another hundred and twenty sermons. And so, when he refers to 'the merits of those who have set their hand to this Song'[103] he must have had these two especially in mind. But there were many others before them.

We should distinguish four distinct methods of interpretation in this long heritage into which John entered. Almost all the christian writers interpreted the Spouse as Christ, but the Bride received various treatments. For Origen each verse was to be interpreted first as the love between Christ and the Church and then as the love between Christ and the individual soul.[104] It seems that he was the first to use this interpretation which became traditional in the East and to some extent in the West. He was followed at the end of the sixth century by St Gregory the Great whose principle of interpretation was: 'what we have said in a general way about the whole Church, we will now apply in a special way to each soul.'[105] As it has been handed down to us, Gregory's work stops abruptly after only eight verses have been dealt with.[106] It seems to me, however, that John owed more to this commentary as regards method of interpretation than to any other writer.

The second type of exposition is that employed by Bede the Venerable.[107] His commentary, which also had a great influence in the West, is almost entirely ecclesiological. 'This is the Song of Songs,' he wrote, 'in which that wise King Solomon describes the mysteries of Christ and his Church, namely the eternal King and his City, under the figure of the Spouse and his Bride. When you read it you should remember that the whole assembly of the elect is called the Church in a general way.'[108] He follows this principle throughout his commentary with only a very brief interest in the spiritual life of the individual. This 'allegorical' interpretation was also given by a number of lesser known writers such as Alcuin,

Haimo of Auxerre, John of Mantua and others. One
should note especially the work of Robert of Tombelaine
who continued the incomplete commentary of Gregory
the Great, while placing much more stress on the
ecclesiological meaning. Since it was in this extended form
that Gregory's commentary was known in the twelfth
century, Robert's influence on later writers was in fact
considerable.[109]

During the twelfth century there were many commentators, notably among the Cistercians, who followed a
third method. These authors tended to concentrate on the
'moral' interpretation, that is to say as an expression of
the love between Christ and the individual soul. Perhaps
the most famous exponent of this method was St Bernard.[110] In his commentary there is only a minimal interest
in the ecclesiological meaning in spite of the fact that
more than half of the eighty six sermons conclude with a
doxology referring to Christ as the Spouse of the Church.
Thus in Sermon 7 he gives the principle that will be the
main line of his interpretation: *'Let him kiss me with the
kiss of his mouth,* she said. Now who is this "she"? The
Bride. And who is the bride? She is the soul thirsting for
God'.[111] So, too, William of St Thierry, Bernard's friend,
concentrates on this 'moral' meaning, interpreting the
Song as a dialogue 'between Christ and the Christian
soul.'[112] With their penetrating insights both these authors
enter deeply into the height of mystical experience.
Other writers who followed Bernard's method, but without
his genius, were Gilbert of Hoyland, Isaac of Stella and
Thomas the Cistercian. This was the method of Richard of
St Victor, too, whom John of Ford mentions as one of his
chief sources, though I have been unable to find any clear
or direct dependence on Richard's *Explicatio in Cantica
Canticorum*[113] in John's sermons.

Finally there are the mariological commentaries. Rupert
of Deutz was one of the first to base his whole commentary

on this method.[114] Several other writers during the
twelfth century also used this interpretation to a greater
or lesser extent, possibly inspired by the application of
verses from the Song to Mary in the liturgy. Perhaps Alain
of Lille in his own mariological commentary has the best
statement of the principle on which this interpretation is
based: 'The Song of love, Solomon's bridal song, refers in a
special and spiritual way to the Church. It should, however, be applied in a very special and in the most spiritual
way to the glorious virgin Mary. With God's approval we
will explain it in this way to the best of our ability.'[115]
John of Ford's commentary is certainly not dominated
by mariology, but he has several long passages in praise of
Mary[116] whom he calls 'the principal bride of Jesus' since
she is the 'chief and highest exemplar of love'.[117]

TEACHING

To understand John's message we must grasp the principles
on which he bases his commentary. It was not meant to be
a theological treatise. He explicitly rejected any attempt to
discuss theological matters in a merely speculative way,
since in his eyes this would lead to irreverence and a
lessening in charity.[118] His intention was entirely practical:
to lead souls to the love of God. If his thought occasionally touches on a speculative theme it is only when this
was necessary to further his principal intention or to
defend himself against censure.[119] As abbot, and therefore
as pastor of souls, he had the duty of teaching his monks
the way to wisdom and spiritual maturity, to the mystical
union with God. To do this he placed before them the
example of the marriage union between the Spouse and
the Bride. For John, as I have said, the Spouse is invariably
identified with Jesus Christ; and the word *sponsa,* the
Bride, can refer either to the Church which is 'the first and

chief Bride of Christ'[120] or to 'any soul united to Christ
in love.'[121]

It will be convenient, then, to summarize John's teaching under four headings: the Spouse Jesus Christ; the
Church his Bride; the soul striving to become the bride of
the Word; and finally, the union of love binding the soul
to the Word.

## 1.  *The beauty of Jesus Christ, the Spouse*

John of Ford's thought may be called spiritual theology,
that is to say theology in its genuine and original sense. He
proposes the 'beauty of the Spouse' to the contemplation
of his readers. In order to give some system to the development of his thought he considers in one place 'the fourfold
glory of the Beloved'[122] and in another place 'the threefold beauty of Jesus'.[123] This glory arises from the fact
that the man Jesus has been raised to union with the Word
of God, and from the union there flows a unique beauty.
It is a beauty beyond all other beauty for 'the Son of the
Virgin was assumed by the form of God to the Only-
begotten of the Father in a manner worthy of his
divinity, and he was glorified in a wonderful way by that
form and from it.'[124] It is our privilege that we too have
been raised to be sons of God in Jesus. But his sonship is
more glorious than ours for he is the Son of God by the
grace of the sacred union by which he is united to the
Only-begotten in the unity of his person.[125]

John of Ford often makes some allusion to the doctrine
that man was made to God's image and likeness. The man
Jesus was not merely made *to* God's image, however, he *is*
God's Image.[126] It follows from this that all other men
approach God only in so far as they conform to this
Image.[127] The image of God, lost at the Fall, is re-formed
in us to the extent that we have this most perfect seal of

God's image impressed on us.[128] It is the whole man, Jesus Christ, who was assumed into the fullness of grace and truth when God poured out on him the complete glory of his divinity.[129] John of Ford insists that this was not simply a union of an indeterminate humanity, so to speak, with the Word, but rather that this specific human flesh was united to the Word of God. Christ's glory consists primarily in the fact that 'this man was assumed into the glorious union of the Word',[130] 'into the unity of one Person', and thus has glory equal with the Father.[131] And yet, of course, this took place at the moment of Jesus' conception, for 'at the same moment as the Only-begotten of God became the son of man, the son of man became the Only-begotten of God'.[132]

From this union there flowed unique privileges. Christ's soul was endowed with full wisdom and perfect righteousness, and indeed with all the infinite riches of God's treasury. His sacred body received an abundant innocence and perfect holiness. It is precisely because of this union and these privileges that Jesus is the cause and exemplar of our salvation.[133] He is for us 'the form of our charity',[134] 'the cause of our salvation',[135] the example of holiness.[136] Christ's love for his Father and for men is clearly the central theme of these sermons. Indeed echoing St John's First Epistle, John tells us that the Spouse is love.[137] The eternal love of Christ is therefore the cause and form of our love of God and our neighbour, for we can only love God because he first loved us.[138] Yet the words *forma, causa* and *exemplum* express more than exemplary causality.[139] No doubt Christ is the form and exemplar of all the virtues,[140] but he is so because he has the form 'in which he is equal to the Father'[141] since he is 'the form and Image of God the Father'.[142] In this context the word 'form' conveys the idea of the nature or essence of a thing. To say that Jesus was 'assumed by the form of God'[143] is to say that he was assumed by God, but it also implies that this 'form' was in some way impressed like a seal on his human nature so that he was endowed 'with the complete form of mercy and the Image of the divine goodness',[144] and that he makes others participate in this form according to their capacity. So he is 'the cause and form of humility' and of all the other virtues especially charity.[145]

To show the close connection between these words we need only consider the phrase where John of Ford tells us that the bride 'takes her example from the form of Christ.'[146] Because Christ is the Word made flesh he is endowed with God's infinite treasures. He is therefore the example that we must imitate.[147] By imitating him we participate in divine light, we return to our origin and we have the exemplar or seal impressed on us.[148] Christ is the archetype and exemplary cause of our spiritual life[149] precisely because he has within himself the fullness of the divinity. This is expressed in scriptural language by saying that Wisdom has been poured out fully on him and that in comparison with this abundant gift we receive only the distilled drops of wisdom.[150] But as the gift is from him, as it is a sharing in his abundance, he is the example that we must imitate.[151]

Not surprisingly, John of Ford sees Christ's death on the cross as the supreme moment of this form and example of love. It was Christ's greatest glory to have humiliated himself utterly and to have taken the form of a slave.[152] 'The *exinanitio* of the Incarnation was not really an abasement, for he who emptied himself remains the splendour, the figure, the image of the Father. This personal dignity gives to the kenosis its character of extraordinary humility, but not of abasement, because it remains bound to a grandeur that is not lost.'[153] But the Father's eternal decree was not merely that his Son should become man but that he should also take on himself the sins of all mankind and expiate them in his blood.[154] Thus the manner of Redemption, i.e. by Christ's passion and death, is seen as an integral part of God's preordained will which was the efficient cause of his passion according to St Thomas,[155] but which John describes in more dramatic terms in Sermon 10. Justice demanded expiation. Man's sin was so great that only the Son of God could expiate it: this was the decree of divine justice. But was it really justice, asks John of Ford, that the innocent one should die for the guilty? Yes indeed, he replies, for 'your love is your Justice. Thus it was in the truest sense your justice to hand over your only Son as a ransom for us all, and it was the justice of that only Son of yours freely to obey his Father's will, so lovingly and effectively. At your command he pursued even unto death the iniquity of mankind, so hateful to your holiness; he affixed it with him to the cross, and utterly removed it from your sight by his blood.'[156] This ultimate humiliation of Christ is the form,[157] the cause and the example of our salvation.[158]

We have seen very briefly the beauty coming to Christ, the man assumed by the Word, and the beauty of the Word, and the beauty of the privileges flowing therefrom to his humanity. It remains necessary to complete this by describing the beauty of Christ in his Bride, the Church.[159]

## 2. The Church, the Bride of Christ[160]

Many of these sermons conclude with a doxology invoking Jesus Christ as the Spouse of the Church, *sponsus ecclesiae.* The most fundamental principle of John's ecclesiology, then, is that Christ is the Spouse of the Church and the Church is the Bride of Christ. Again and again throughout his commentary he returns to the theme of the unique bond of love uniting Christ to the Church. At the end of two remarkable sermons on the infinite love between the Father, the Son and the Holy Spirit—a love that is the origin and final end of all love—he asserts that the whole purpose and aim of the Church is to rest finally in 'this end without end, always glorifying the most sublime and unique unity of the Blessed Trinity in its wonderfully incomprehensible love . . . . '[161] It goes without saying that this love with which God loves the Church is in every respect more perfect than the love with which the Church loves God. Yet John uses the idea to record in detail every aspect of this love.[162]

The union between Christ and his Church is a marriage bond. The glory proper to the Church comes from the fact that 'Christ joined it to himself in a bond of marriage'.[163] By this insistence on a marriage of love, the Old Testament bond between God and the unfaithful Jewish people (a bond that rested on the justice of the Law and was rescinded by Christ) is implicitly contrasted with the new marriage between Christ and the Church of the Gentiles, a bond resting on grace and love.

In a sense the whole of salvation history before the coming of Christ can be looked on as a preparation for this marriage of love. From the time of Adam until the birth of Christ the Church was in the penumbra of dawn, rising out of the darkness. This period prepared the world for the true Light. The prophets and their teaching gave greater firmness to the faith of the apostles and the early Church. It was a period that constantly looked forward in type and prophecy to the Church which could only come to birth when the true and full Light shone out on the world.[164] So John of Ford saw 'the woman coming from the side of the man' as the type of the Church.

Every action of Christ's life has a sacramental character for all future time, and many of his acts were the direct fulfilment of prophecy.[165] Yet the outstanding moment of Redemption is precisely his death. A long tradition

witnesses to the birth of the Church from the side of
Christ on the cross when the marriage of Christ and his
Church was as it were solemnized: ' . . . the Church was
formed in the womb of your compassion from your own
flesh and bone; it came forth from your side which was the
source of the marriage bond and of nuptial love.'[166] The
Jewish people, the Synagogue, opened the side of the dead
Christ so that the Church of the Gentiles might enter it, be
dipped and washed in that saving blood.[167] And yet John
of Ford also repeats the other tradition that speaks of the
Church coming to birth at Pentecost when the Holy Spirit
was poured out on the disciples.[168]

He instinctively used traditional symbols to express
different aspects of the Church's nature. He often refers
to it as a garden, *hortus,* in which Christ nurtures the fruit
and the vines of love; where the Holy Spirit rests in the
souls of the faithful.[169] In another place the Church itself
is the vine, and this vine has spread its shoots over the
whole earth.[170] He is particularly fond of calling the
Church the flock of God, *grex Domini*, with Christ as the
Good Shepherd.[171] Developing one important facet of
this symbol, he goes into great detail about the duties of
shepherds of the flock, i.e. prelates and their pastoral office.[172] Another basic symbol that he often uses is the Mystical Body, especially when he refers to the glory of Christ,
the Head of the Church, but he also brings out the glory
due to the whole Church and to each individual member.

Although the early Church, *ecclesia primitiua*, was frequently set forth as the paradigm or model for all future
ages, the medieval writers make it clear that the Jewish
people had rejected Christ and that the promises made to
them were transferred to the Church of the Gentiles,
*ecclesia gentium*. The early Church was the model of
unity: that marvellous unity between Jews and Gentiles
who were united in one faith and newly wedded to Christ
in love, the unanimity in perfect love between all

members of the Church, their concord in waiting patiently
for the Holy Spirit.[173] But it is precisely the Church of the
Gentiles that is the new Bride of Christ. The call is therefore universal. It embraces all nations and all men 'who
were created to the image of God and have preserved this
image through grace or have repaired it through repentance.'[174]

For the purpose of a sermon the members of the Church
can be neatly divided into categories. Sometimes John
uses the hierarchic division, sometimes the charismatic.
Noah, Daniel and Job in the Old Testament are types of
the hierarchic structure; they represent pastors, religious
and the faithful respectively.[175] Since the Pope is the head
of this hierarchy John of Ford refers to him and also to the
other high ecclesiastical dignitaries in several places. The
Pope is the spokesman or representative of the whole
Church. When Christ spoke to Peter he spoke to the whole
Church, *'quia in Petro responsum est omnibus . . . .* '[176] It
is to the successor of Peter that the Church looks for the
definition and preservation of the purity of doctrine and
faith. The Pope and the hierarchy alone have authority,
power and the ruling office over the Church, and yet they
are at the service of the Church and should give expression
to her belief and love. They should be the bond of unity
within the Church.[177]

John certainly held that the Pope possesses the highest
power both of the priesthood and kingship: 'He has the
totality of royal and priestly power, so that he enjoys the
right of placing the crown on the heads of both kings and
bishops.'[178] He was of course unaware of the conflicts of
faith and loyalty to which this principle would lead very
shortly after his death. But in his own day he had seen the
conflict working itself out first in the murder of Thomas
Becket and later in the Interdict during John's reign.

However that might be, in the final analysis the Church
and all its members are waiting for the sight of God's face

unveiled in heaven 'when we shall be transformed into the image of the Only-begotten of the Father'.[179] The whole Church is hurrying forward, as it were, to this apotheosis of perfect joy. Underlying much of John's thought is this anagogic interpretation of Scripture—the escatological climax to the Church's movement towards its completion in the Kingdom of heaven.

### 3. *The soul that strives for union with the Word.*

John of Ford accepted fully the doctrine that man was made to the image of God. This doctrine rests on the account of man's creation in Genesis, but it received considerable elaboration by the Fathers, especially St Augustine, and was used extensively in the twelfth and thirteenth centuries.[180] He is simply repeating this doctrine when he tells us that 'God planted paradise with trees and placed in it the first man whom he had formed. The rational spirit of man was formed to the image of its Maker'.[181] At the fall Adam did indeed retain this image which cannot be lost, yet he damaged it and he lost the likeness that was connected with it. 'Our first parents seem to have fallen away from their Creator. They were made to his image and likeness and placed over all his works.'[182] At the devil's instigation they lost this likeness, and not just for themselves but for their whole posterity, the human race. Thus the three powers of the soul: memory, reason and will, in which the image and likeness principally reside, became subject to corruption and vice.[183]

Christ came to restore this image and likeness; because he was the perfect Image of God he alone could seal other men with the image.[184] By imitating him they strive to become on the spiritual or moral level a sort of living photographic resemblance to him.[185] The real meaning of life, according to the authors of the twelfth century, is this gradual transformation into the clear image of God.[186]

The bride of the Word is anyone who has gone a long way towards this transformation. Naturally John makes her the ideal for all souls and speaks a great deal about her vision of or union with Christ. But he is even more concerned with those less privileged souls, the *adolescentulae,* who look to the bride for their inspiration and encouragement. In other words he deals not only with the advanced degrees of the spiritual life but also with the first steps of beginners. He maps out the route from the region of unlikeness to the region of likeness, from darkness to light,[187] from error and sin to truth and love, from the absence of the Spouse to the full vision of his eternal presence.[188] There are, for John, four stages in this process: first there are the penitents who have been converted from sin to a life of virtue; then there are the virgins, i.e. those who have undertaken the life of virginity in a religious order; next, those who are striving for holiness and suffer trials patiently for Christ's sake; finally there are those who are burning with love and have frequently been admitted to the kiss of contemplation.[189]

The first stage is marked by self-knowledge and a deep consciousness of personal sin. It is, of course, God who gives us this knowledge of our sinfulness. We learn from this light that shines in our darkness just how far we are from God, and we begin to desire a life of virtue.[190] The dominant theme at this early stage is repentance and humility. The penitent man groans and weeps inwardly, is covered with confusion at the sight of his sins.[191] This type of repentant humility is close to St Bernard's teaching and definition.[192] John of Ford depends on Bernard here for he too distinguishes three degrees: humility towards oneself, towards one's neighbour, and towards God. Moreover, he defines the first degree as 'the most true recognition of oneself'.[193] It implies that we humbly take stock of ourselves and repent of our evil deeds, while we ascribe all

our good actions and tendencies to God.[194] For this
reason humility is the mother of all the virtues,[195] since it
is there at the first beginnings of our conversion to God
and it nurtures our progress through all the stages as the
lost likeness is gradually restored. For this conversion to
become well established we must have frequent recourse to
the purifying waters of repentance. Reborn and washed by
the Holy Spirit in the sacrament of penance the soul begins
to be re-formed to the image of God; the new creature
reappears from under the dirt and grime of sin.[196]

This first stage, marked by repentance and confession
of sins, seems to have been a prerequisite to entry into the
monastery. John of Ford expected the second stage to take
place within the religious life—the life of consecrated virginity. This was entirely in accord with the ideas of his
time. No doubt he would not have denied the possibility
of a deep spiritual life to men and women living in the
world, but he would have expected them to live in a
monastic fashion, striving after monastic virtues. Perhaps
the most characteristic quality in the progress through this
second stage is set out in the meaning given to the word
*aemulatio*—it is a strong desire for holiness, an effort to
imitate the virtues of holy men.[197] John of Ford empha-
sizes that this quest for holiness is a type of love. It can be
called love when it is marked by the struggle to overcome
one's vices and to clothe oneself with virtues.[198] He places
before us the example of the great men in the Old Testament—Moses, David, Elias and the rest.[199] Above all we
should strive to imitate Jesus. Here the chief monastic virtue, obedience, is set before us in the example of Christ
who subjected himself not only to his heavenly Father
but even to his earthly parents, Christ who became
obedient unto death.[200] Once more he insists that the seal
or likeness of God must shine out in our souls: by love in
the will, by prudence in the understanding, by the practice
of virtue and perseverance, until the image begins to

correspond to the only true Image which is Christ.[201]

This holy emulation can be a very demanding thing. It means that we should try to break with all human ties of affection in order to concentrate on the love of God.[202] More positively it is the replacing of merely human love with the two spiritual affections: divine love and hope. These are the two principal affections that enable the person to progress along the road to holiness and to advance in the more excellent way of divine love.[203] He must always keep the journey's end vividly before his eyes. It is hope that impresses the promised reward indelibly on his mind, but it is love that makes him patient and kind as he proceeds on his journey. These two virtues are like the feet of the traveller which move alternately as he strides out energetically along the road.[204]

At this stage of the journey a man needs to sustain himself by meditation. Perhaps reflection would be a better word. John of Ford certainly expected his monks to meditate on the Scripture, and he was himself no mean master of the art. This is the food that he prepared for himself and his monks, something that he used to good effect when phrase after phrase recalls some text in a catena of scriptural allusions.[205] Yet meditation should not be a formal exercise limited to certain periods during the day. He wants us to reflect on the beauty of everyday things which should be seen as symbols pointing to divine realities. He compares mental reflection of this sort to the busy activity of a bee gathering nectar from many flowers and storing it up in honeycombs. The love of Christ tends to increase with the accumulation of good thoughts.[206]

There is no obvious line of demarcation between his second and third stages. He makes the distinction in order to discuss the patient suffering of the martyrs and also the patience of all those who suffer great trials for Christ's sake.[207] The theme of 'patience during suffering' is one on which he loves to dwell, no doubt partly because of the troubles during King John's reign, but more universally because Jesus himself is the model of patience in his suffering and death on the cross.[208] To imitate Jesus in his silence under mockery and torture is to enter the school of his secret philosophy.[209] The practical application of this is that each of us by our life of sin and disobedience has added to the mockery, while Jesus still remains silent, waiting for us to return to our senses, to come back to life.[210] When we have been well-grounded in the teaching of this school we progress in the depth of our silence. True and perfect silence is found in the example of Jesus who was silent not only during the ordinary troubles of life, but more especially under great affliction, and bore all things with the utmost patience and even with joy.[211]

It was customary for Cistercian writers to call the monastery 'the school of Christ', and to contrast it with the schools of the world where rhetoric and dialectic were taught. The monastery was for them the school of love,[212] the school of humility and silence.[213] Here they could acquire knowledge, but not the knowledge that makes a man wise in his own eyes. It is the knowledge of the saints, the knowledge given to the pure in heart.[214] This is the true philosophy, drawn from the experience of close contact with God who infuses light and understanding into the minds of his lovers and takes away their ignorance and hardness of heart.[215] In this school one gives oneself to the study of the truth that is Christ, a study that has as its aim the love and imitation of Christ.[216] It is a study based on the practical exercise of virtues and results in a deep knowledge of the mysteries of Christ.[217]

During this stage of his progress a man has an increasing insight into his own distance from perfection. This is only another way of saying that he gains a deepening knowledge of Christ. He is striving to live a virtuous life but experience teaches him that he has still a long way to go. An increase

in his awareness of his own weakness shows him clearly
the truth about himself; how far he still is from wisdom
and perfection, how far from the steps of perfect man.
Yet this very realization of self and sinfulness is a light
shining in the darkness: 'I may be ignorant of myself, but
provided I know that I do not know, provided my sickness is clearly before me, I am helped and strengthened by
it . . . . For the true preparation for seeing you, O Lord, is
to know myself'.[218] This knowledge should make a man
eager to cut out of his life all unlawful pleasures, all care
for merely earthly pursuits, all carnal desire.[219] That is its
negative aspect. On the positive side it brings him into contact with the treasures of knowledge, the riches of
immortality, and the likeness of God that is found in
Jesus,[220] for in him alone are the infinite treasures of
God's wisdom and knowledge.[221] In many places wisdom
and knowledge are set in juxtaposition like this.[222]
Wisdom is in fact the end we should aim at, while
knowledge is one of the means to that end. Knowledge is
to wisdom what the light of the moon is to the light of the
sun. Knowledge is a lesser light. When a man has the spirit
of knowledge he still remains to some extent in the night
of unknowing. Yet this is a stage to the fuller light of
wisdom.[223]

The bride possesses wisdom, but she communicates
knowledge to the young maidens. That is to say, in this
stage we look to deeply spiritual persons not for the teaching of doctrine or the expounding of speculative theology,
but quite simply for their understanding of the love of
Jesus—a knowledge that surpasses every other type of
knowledge.[224] Christ is the Wisdom of God. From the
bride we can learn to appreciate him as the Wisdom that is
the creator and artificer of all things, the one who possesses all knowledge, and disperses the dark cloud of
ignorance in which we are all wrapped.[225]

But if these authors call the monastery a school they

also refer to it as a desert. Indeed it is a threefold desert.[226] These three deserts correspond in a broad way to the traditional three ways of the spiritual life: purgation, illumination, union. For John of Ford says that in the first desert we are purged from vices, in the second we are invited to begin the climb towards perfection, in the third—the target of our efforts and ascent—we rest on the top of the mountain of perfection.

## 4. *The Bride of the Word.*

This journey towards God enters its final stage when the soul is filled with the spirit of wisdom.[227] Wisdom is in fact the goal of perfection. As such it is identified with pure love of God and is necessarily joined to a deep experience of God.[228] So the soul that has been given this spirit of wisdom and has experienced a certain intense contemplation becomes a bride of the Word, *sponsa Verbi.* A bride of the Word may be defined as 'any soul that cleaves to the Lord Jesus with all her love'[229] and 'embraces him with a devotion that is entire and undivided.'[230]

Although John of Ford, as St Bernard before him, uses expressions proper to married love to portray the union between the Church and Christ, he preserves some of his most intimate, most beautiful phrases for the person who is united to the Word as his bride. It is a marriage union initiated in joy and fear. 'When the soul sees herself now wedded to the Word, her joy is mingled with fear and trembling, for she is afraid that there might be found in her something unbecoming, something displeasing to such royal majesty.'[231] Yet as this spiritual marriage continues, it is the union of love that is stressed more and more exclusively: 'I am made one with the Beloved, I am conformed to him, I am totally within him, and I have become one spirit with him.'[232] This last phrase, a quotation from

St Paul, is used by John of Ford at least fourteen times to express the highest degree of the spiritual life. Union with the Word in the most intense love possible is characteristic of this stage. The bride is trapped and held fast by the violent bond of holy desire. She is attracted to Christ by love, blissful in her marriage with him, united with him in one spirit.[233]

If the medieval writers use some sexual imagery to express the intimacy of the union, it is because they need this to bring out more vividly some of its essential attributes. Thus they can say that the bride becomes pregnant by the power of the Holy Spirit and receives from him the blessed seed that is the sweet love of Christ.[234] But we find immediately that the writer intends to present the movement from the slow and laborious task of meditation to the delightfully spontaneous act of contemplation.[235] It could be said that the spiritual marriage, like an ordinary human marriage, has two ends: the union of love between the soul and the Word, and the fecundity of gaining souls to Christ. The bride of the Word gives herself entirely to him for these two ends, for 'she carefully devotes her life to him in love and she is fruitful in forming souls to his likeness.'[236]

This union finds its chief expression in contemplation. Commenting on the various ways by which the bride progresses on her journey, John of Ford says: 'Sometimes she goes out to care for the young maidens, sometimes she comes back to look after herself, sometimes she enters into herself to contemplate her Spouse and this is her chief duty.'[237] He nowhere gives a strict definition of contemplation, however. Perhaps the closest he gets to this is when he talks about the sleep of the soul: 'The bride sleeps when in the contemplation of God she withdraws her mind from all the changing things in this world and goes out from herself to taste only the things that are above.'[238]

Richard of St Victor defines contemplation as a deep

insight in which the mind is fixed in wonder on heavenly mysteries.[239] John echoes this idea when he says that the person who is a bride feels herself lifted up to God with joy and wonder.[240] Indeed it is a state of soul often called a vision. It is a vision of Christ's face,[241] of the eternal light,[242] of the glory of God.[243] It is a clear and penetrating intuition of God's wisdom and goodness, and it embraces the profound mysteries of Jesus' love—the infinite love of the Spouse who is at the same time Incarnate Wisdom of the Father.[244] In these and many other places John sees contemplation as a type of vision and light. 'The Spouse,' he insists, 'is light and his face is wholly shining with light like the sun.'[245]

Even in the earlier stages there is a kind of vision that is not fully spiritual, consisting as it does in the knowledge of Christ in his human nature. Here the soul may have a certain intimacy with the Word clothed in flesh; this can indeed even be called a face to face vision of God in human flesh. John stresses moreover that this type of vision can develop or deepen until it becomes only a step from the vision of ineffable light that will be seen in heaven.[246]

Something of this latter vision seems to have been granted to the mystics, if only transiently. It brings with it a deep feeling of wonder, yet at that same time a certain awe or fear that it may be spoiled or soiled by sin. The person who experiences this vision finds his evil tendencies melting away under the warm fire of his attachment to Jesus. Joy and spiritual exaltation totally possess him. 'Oh how lovely is this face, more desirable than anything else in the world.'[247] After a sudden thrill of delight at the memory of a personal experience of this sort, John soberly warns us about its brevity: 'However, this solemn feast, this glory is only for an hour; that is to say, it will only be for a brief time and at rare intervals. Yes, but how essential the work of this hour, for Jesus in his turn glorifies the person who renders him glory. This vision of Jesus' face is truly a time of salvation, a life-giving action. Anyone who sees his face will instantly die to himself and live for Jesus alone. Happy are those eyes, happy are all who have caught sight of this vision.'[248]

Yet mystical wisdom is not dominated by vision. John puts at least an equal stress on the fire and warmth of love. 'The heart of the bride grows warm with admiration at the immense love of Jesus.'[249] Or, in a different imagery, it is a scented garden of aromatic plants where the bride breathes the fragrance of her Beloved.[250] To describe this aspect of mystical union he uses words like *osculum, amplexus, uisitatio*, words that are more associated with the warmth of affection and love than with intellectual perception. At the outset the quest for wisdom is marked by a humble introspection stemming from an increased awareness of sin. Soon, however, this gives place to serenity as pardon is granted, and grace and kindly mercy are felt to be present. When all the preparatory work has been done, God may raise the bride to higher things so that 'she will merit to hear the hidden words of God.'[251] The Word of God becomes present to the bride and speaks words that cannot be uttered. They are words of love, words which only the Word can whisper, and only to his bride. 'These are words of paradise; and in paradise there is nothing more ineffable than these loving words, these secret, hidden words.'[252]

During this 'visit' by the Word the bride enters into a deep nuptial conversation, *nuptiale alloquium*, which is beyond the powers of human expression to describe. It takes place when she merits that long-desired kiss of the Word—'when she experiences those unbelievable embraces and becomes one spirit with the Only-begotten of God through the power of the Holy Spirit.'[253] This 'visit' is the highest good that can be received in this life. The bride's mind and will become fully captive to the love of God so that nothing remains in her that love has not conquered.[254] It is as though the barrier dividing her from the Spouse had been removed; she is now ready for the secret mysteries of God, ready for 'eternal light and the spirit of grace'.[255]

When this stage is complete a new kind of serenity pervades the soul and it becomes transformed into the image of God.[256] This moment is 'the fruition of divine love, a foretaste of the glory of heaven.'[257] Anything that has marred the likeness to God is completely purged away. The soul is re-formed in the image by the Word who is the express Image of the Father,[258] just as the iron in the fire glows white-hot with the fire.[259] In this state the soul moves from strength to strength. The beauty that was hers at the beginning of her marriage increases imperceptibly under the influence of her continual contemplation.[260] In the end her likeness to the Word is perfect. It is this perfection that John of Ford calls 'the glorious transformation into the image of God.'[261]

We cannot leave it there. The bride is not only transformed in herself, she is also fruitful towards others. The two themes of spiritual motherhood and pastoral care for souls have an essential place in John's thought. He tells us that the bride spiritually conceives and bears children to the image and likeness of Christ.[262] It is her duty to love them with maternal affection so that through her the love of Christ may be formed in them.[263] She instructs them in devotion and the things necessary for salvation rather than in the subtle speculations of intellectuals.[264] Thus anyone who has the office of caring for souls and instructing them in the love of God is entitled to be called a 'mother of Jesus'.[265] In one place at least John seems to consider the pastoral ministry higher than the contemplative life, namely when he puts in the first rank of merit 'those who are called to rule over souls and perform this ministry chastely and diligently.'[266] He points out that they should not seek their own glory or personal riches but only

Christ's glory in the procreation and upbringing of spiritual children. He intends to place them higher than contemplatives, it seems clear from the context, only when they have in fact attained a high degree of perfection and are well accustomed to a life of contemplation.[267]

CONCLUSION

I have only been able to touch briefly on a few of the more important themes used by John of Ford. Enough has been said, however, to give some indication of his place in the history of spirituality. On the one hand he seems to be entirely uninfluenced by the scholastic method beginning to dominate Western thought during his lifetime and reaching its zenith only a few years after his death. We should remember that St Dominic's campaign against the Albigenses began in 1206 while John was still alive, though there is no indication that he had heard of it, and in fact he appears to have given up hope of victory over this heresy.[268] Albert the Great was born at the beginning of the thirteenth century and Thomas Aquinas about twelve years after John's death. On the other hand he inherited from the early Cistercian fathers many themes dear to all the spiritual writers of the Middle Ages. Chronologically he comes somewhere between them and the English mystics, although in his approach he is closer to the earlier writers.

It is unlikely that these sermons were well known during the thirteenth and fourteenth centuries. I have been unable to discover any direct dependence on them among the English mystics. Certainly the scarcity of manuscripts, of which there is now only one still extant, reflects this. And yet, this does less than justice to his thought. In spite of a certain amplitude or even prolixity, many of these sermons are surely equal to anything written by Guerric of Igny or

Gilbert of Hoyland. For example, the fine *Sermon 14* is a profound meditation on the mystery of the Trinity and sufficient in itself to establish John as a theologian of considerable weight. It would be difficult to find its match in anything written by, say, Richard Rolle among the English mystics. In fact, part of the special quality of John's thought is his mastery over the balance between a deep spiritual theology (as in the sermon just mentioned) and his equally profound theological spirituality; between his insights into the Church as the Bride of Christ, or the other mysteries of the faith, and his insistence on the spiritual life of the individual. He is a master of the spiritual life. He knows how to lead the beginner along the hesitant path at the outset of his journey, and at the same time, having apparently had some personal experience of the heights of mystical contemplation, he is also able to direct the more advanced person.

There is, then, in these sermons much that will be spiritually rewarding, much that is profound, and much for the student of theology and spirituality. This is why it is particularly pleasing to present John of Ford to English readers, so that for the first time his teaching may be fully appreciated and he may take his rightful place in the history of early English spirituality.

*Hilary Costello*

*Mount Saint Bernard*
*Coalville, Leicester*

# NOTES

## INTRODUCTION

1.    For much of this Introduction I am particularly indebted to Dr. C. J. Holdsworth who allowed me to use his unpublished doctoral thesis: *Learning and Literature of English Cistercians, 1167–1214, with special reference to John of Ford.* This thesis certainly gives the most detailed and extensive account of John of Ford's life and work that has been written.

2.    Forde Abbey is now in Dorset since the county boundaries were revised in 1846.

3.    Dom Maurice Bell, ed., *Wulfric of Haselbury, by John, Abbot of Ford,* Somerset Record Society, 47, (1933).

4.    Bell p. xviii, affirms 'that the life of St Wulfric was begun soon after 1180' and 'finished in 1185 or 1186'. But Holdsworth, *Learning and Literature* pp. 98–102, suggests the much earlier date for the commencement of the work and he also brings evidence to indicate that John of Ford could still have been working on it during the 1190s.

5.    Holdsworth, pp. 100–101.

6.    Oliver, *Monasticon Exoniense*, p. 338.

7.    Janauschek, *Originum Cisterciensium* (Vienna, 1877) pp. 40–41. For Waverly see *ibid.* pp. 16–17. For the name-places of Cistercian Houses, dates of foundation and county location, I have always consulted *Medieval Religious Houses: England and Wales,* by David Knowles and R. Neville Hadcock (London, 1953) pp. 104–121, corrected according to the new information in *Additions and Corrections to Medieval Religious Houses: England and Wales,*

in the *English Historical Review* 72 (1957) 60–87.

8.    *Baudouin de Ford, Le sacrement de l'autel,* introduction par J. Leclercq, texte latin établi par J. Morson, traduction française par E. de Solms; Sources chrétiennes, 93 (Paris 1963) pp. 7–9. *Cf.* Holdsworth, pp. 49–62.

9.    PL 204, 403–774.

10.    C. H. Talbot, 'The Verses of Roger of Ford on Our Lady', *Coll.,* 6 (1939) 44–54. *See* also C. J. Holdsworth, 'John of Ford and English Cistercian Writing 1167–1214', Transactions of the Royal Historical Society 11 (1961) pp. 125–126.

11.    Bell, cap. 50.

12.    *Annales Monastici,* ed. Luard. (Rolls Series 36); *Annales de Margam,* p. 21, under the year 1191: 'Johannes abbas de Bynnadone factus est abbas de Forda'. On the same page under the year 1190, there is an entry to the effect that the previous abbot, Robert, had died: 'Obiit Fredericus imperator, et Baldewinus archiepiscopus, et Robertus abbas de Forda.'

13.    *Statuta Capitulorum Generalium Ordinis Cisterciensis,* ed. J. M. Canivez, tome I (Louvain, 1933); *Statuta* 1198, 43, p. 230.

14.    *Statuta* 1199, 31; p. 238.

15.    *Ibid.* 66; p. 245.

16.    *Annales monast.* I; *Annales de Margam,* p. 25–26: 'In die Assumptionis sanctae Mariae apud Fordam, praesentibus dominis abbatibus, Johanne de Waverlege, et Johanne de Forde, et domino Willelmo Brewere, eligitur conventus xii. monachorum, praefecto eis viro industrio Gregorio, ad construendam abbatiam de Dunkeswelle'. And on the same page it is stated that this group set out on 16 November. Knowles and Hadcock, *Medieval Religious Houses,* p. 108. Cf *Annales Monast.* II; *Annales de Waverleia,* p. 253, sub anno 1201: 'Dunkewelle fundata est'.

17.   *Statuta* 1201, 43, p. 272.

18.   S. F. Hockey, *Quarr Abbey and its Lands 1132–1631* (Leicester University Press, 1970) pp. 6, 14.

19.   *Ibid.* pp. 34–35.

20.   *Statuta* 1202, 34; p. 281.

21.   *Ibid.* 35, p. 281.

22.   D. Knowles, *The Monastic Order in England* (Cambridge, 1941) p. 660. Cf *Statuta* 1184, 15, p. 97; 1192, 16, p. 149; 1195, 66, p. 191; 1196, 8, p. 199.

23.   *Statuta* 1202, 36; p. 281: 'Prior autem et cellerarius et alii officiales qui contradicere praesumpserint de domibus propriis emittantur, nonnisi per generale Capitulum reversuri. Item dicitur de conversis.'

24.   *Statuta* 1205, 54; p. 318.

25.   *Ibid.* 1204, 3; p. 295.

26.   *Ibid.* 1205, 55; p. 318.

27.   Holdsworth, *Learning and Literature,* p. 82; Knowles and Hadcock, *Medieval Religious Houses,* p. 112.

28.   *Statuta* 1206, 23; p. 324.

29.   D. Knowles, *The Monastic Order in England,* p. 659–660. James S. Donnelly, *The Decline of the Medieval Cistercian Lay-brotherhood,* History Series no. 3 (Fordham University Press, 1949) p. 28–32. David H. Williams, *The Welsh Cistercians* (Pontypool, 1969) p. 54. *Statuta* 1195, 76 and 77; 193.

30.   *Statuta* 1210, 42; p. 377.

31.   *Ibid.* 1213, 64; pp. 416–417.

32.   *Ibid.* 1214, 40; p. 425; 1215, 41; p. 443.

33. C. J. Holdsworth, 'John of Ford and the Interdict,' *The English Historical Review* 78 (1963) pp. 705-714; *Learning and Literature,* pp. 87-94. W. L. Warren, *King John* (Penguin Books, 1966) pp. 185 and 189. A.D., 'John of Ford,' *Cîteaux* 21 (1970) pp. 105-110, but this article is inaccurate in several important details.

34. Sermon 76, 235-238.

35. Holdsworth, *Learning and Literature,* p. 84, gives several details from the Pipe Rolls to confirm this fact.

36. Sermon 76, 239-242.

37. *Statuta* 1203, 15, p. 287. *Pipe Roll 6 John:* 'Abbas de Forde debet j m.' p. 83.

38. Sermon 41, 207-210.

39. *Selected Letters of Pope Innocent III concerning England* (1198-1216), edited by C. R. Cheney and W. H. Semple (London, 1953) p. 96. Cf C. R. Cheney, 'King John and the Papal Interdict,' *Bulletin of John Rylands Library,* 31 (1945) p. 295.

40. Sermon 41, 239-240.

41. Sermon 76, 219-269.

42. Cheney and Semple, *Selected Letters,* nos. 45, pp. 130-136 and 70, pp. 188-190.

43. *Ibid.* p. 188: 'This led to the relaxation of the Interdict on 2 July'. Mass was celebrated at Tewkesbury Abbey on 5 July: 'Nos incepimus divina celebrare iii. non. Julii'; *Annales Monast.* II; *Annales de Theokesberia,* p. 61 sub anno 1214.

44. *Annales monasterii de Waverleia; Annales Monast.* II (Rolls Series 36) pp. 281-82 sub anno 1214: 'Obiit Johannes abbas de Forda, xi. kal. Maii; successit Rogerus, supprior ejusdem loci.' In the *Curia Regis Roll 15-16 John,* p. 301-302, for the same year, there is mention of an abbot Robert of Ford, but this must presumably be a mistake for abbot Roger.

45.  J. Leland, *Commentarii de Scriptoribus Britannicis* I (Oxford, 1709) p. 231.

46.  Guerric of Igny, *Liturgical Sermons,* vols 1 and 2, Cistercian Fathers Series nos. 8 (1970) and 32 (1971); Introduction pp. xviii-xxiii. Guerric comments on a verse of the Song in 'The Second Sermon for Saints Peter and Paul' (vol. 2, p. 153); 'The Third Sermon for Saints Peter and Paul' (2, p. 160); 'The Second Sermon for the Assumption' (2, p. 173); and 'A Sermon for Arousing Devotion at Psalmody' (2, p. 213).

47.  Holdsworth, *Learning and Literature,* pp. 111–116.

48.  Bell, *Wulfric of Haselbury,* Introduction p. xix.

49.  Sermons 6, 1; 43, 1; 91, 1; 106, 1; 112, 1.

50.  89, 12; 90, 10; 97, 11; 102, 11; 112, 12.

51.  11, 8; 39, Incipit. 1; 94, 12; 112, 12.

52.  106, 13; cf 118, 9.

53.  Prologue, 1. 5. 6; 39, 1.

54.  Prologue, 2. 5; cf. 10, 1.

55.  Guerric of Igny, *Liturgical Sermons,* vol. 1 (CF 8), Introduction p. xix–xx.

56.  39, 1: 'Scio autem quia nonnullis in tractu priori diffusior uisus sim . . . . '

57.  *Guerric d'Igny, Sermons,* tome 1, Sources Chrétiennes no. 166 (Paris, 1970) Introduction p. 74–77.

58.  8, 4.

59.  8, note referring to line 85 of the latin text.

60.  16, 9.

61.    6, 6.

62.    Guerric of Igny, *Liturgical Sermons,* vol. 1, p. 37.

63.    114, 7.

64.    36, 5; 41, 1; 67, 12.

65.    88, 3.

66.    11, 4.

67.    10, 3-5.

68.    25, 6; 69, 6.

69.    88, 9.

70.    12, 3. 4.

71.    24, 2.

72.    74, 4; 77, 3.

73.    For example 41, 9; 65, 10.

74.    8, 4.

75.    24, 2.

76.    97, 4 quoting Aristotle's *De animalibus* iv, 10 either directly or, more likely, from another source: *cf* Holdsworth, 'John of Ford and Early Cistercian Writing,' p. 124.

77.    57, 1; cf 60, 1 and 85, 7.

78.    For example, in Sermon 60 after a brief reference to the literal meaning he refers back to the previous sermon and says: 'We have discussed, as far as the Lord enabled us, how these same words applied to the Spouse. Now, with your love, let us see, by God's grace, how they can also be applied to the Bride'. He then applies them to the Church.

79.    'But now the text is to be taken as meaning her who has deserved to be married to the heavenly Bridegroom, through the singular privilege of true love . . . . '

80.    For example, Sermons 50 and 51; 52 and 53; 54 and 55.

81.    One can also speak of the four senses of Scripture by including the anagogical sense: The question has been thoroughly investigated by Henri De Lubac, *Exégèse Médiévale: les quatres sens de l'écriture;* première partie, tome 1 (Aubier, 1959).

82.    42, 2; 53, 1; 112, 10.

83.    62, 1; 90, 6.

84.    53, 4.

85.    62, 1: *'Prima facies sermonis.'*

86.    In Sermon 15, 2 it is called the *'superficies'* and *'superficies litteralis'*. To understand the real meaning of the Scriptures we must 'enter into the inner-room of wisdom', i.e. into the allegorical meaning, and this is dealt with in paragraph 3 and those following. Elsewhere it is referred to as the *'litterae superficies'* (46, 2; 54, 1).

87.    54, 1. 'But this literal rind is an external thing and very dry. If a little one should thoughtlessly eat it, he would come up against the death-dealing letter.' See also 25, 3; 82, 3.

88.    Hilary Costello, 'The Idea of the Chuch in the Sermons of John of Ford, *Cîteaux*, 21 (1970) pp. 239-240.

89.    Henri De Lubac, *Exégèse Médiévale* 1: 498-511.

90.    5, 2.

91.    72, 6.

92.    Prologue, 3.

93.    50, 11; See also 49, 10; 58, 1.

94.    114, 6; 120, 6.

95.    Hilary Costello, 'John of Ford and the Quest for Wisdom,' Cîteaux 23 (1972) pp. 141–159.

96.    Prologue, 4.

97.    54, 2. 5; 55, 1. 9.

98.    54, 4: ' . . . and what a great vocation, what more glorious title, than to be called kings or queens of heaven. Concubines, indeed, have the glory of a lower dignity, but it is enough for them.' Cf 55, 8: 'But concubines possess less of the spirit of understanding . . . . ' It seems clear from the context that the 'concubines' are those religious who do not have the care of souls.

99.    Prologue, 2.

100. *Ibid.* 1. 4.

101. St Bernard, *Sermones super cantica canticorum,* OB 1 (1957) and 2 (1958), edd. J. Leclercq, C. H. Talbot, and H. M. Rochais (Rome: Editiones cistercienses). For the date of composition see vol. I, Introduction p. xv.

102. Gilbert of Hoyland, *Sermones in canticum salomonis,* PL 184, 11–252. For the date of his death, see E. Mikkers, 'De vita et operibus Gilberti de Hoylandia,' *Cîteaux* 14 (1963) p. 42. There are indeed forty-eight sermons in the Migne edition but Sermons 11 and 12 should be combined as in the manuscripts. This is indicated by Fr Mikkers, p. 272.

103. Prologue, 4.

104. Origen, *The Song of Songs: Commentary and Homilies,* translated and annotated by R. P. Lawson, Ancient Christian Writers 26 (London, 1957) Introduction pp. 10–16. See also pp. 59–60.

105. *Expositio in canticum canticorum,* ed. P. Verbracken, 144 (1963) p. 17, no. 15, lines 305–306.

106. *Ibid.,* Introduction, p. viii.

107. *In cantica canticorum;* PL 91, 1079–1222.

108. *Ibid.,*

109. Robert of Tombelaine, *Super cantica canticorum expositio,* PL 79, 492–548. See *Expositio,* CCh 144, Introduction, p. viii-ix.

110. The Works of Bernard of Clairvaux 2: *On the Song of Songs* I (CF 4, 1971) translated by Kilian Walsh, introduction by M. Corneille Halflants.

111. *Ibid.,* Sermon 7, 2, p. 38 (I have modified the translation slightly).

112. The Works of William of St Thierry: *Exposition on the Song of Songs* (CF 6, 1970) translated by Mother Columba Hart, introduction by J. M. Dechanet, p. 7.

113. PL 196, 405–524.

114. Rupert of Deutz, *In cantica canticorum: de incarnatione Domini,* PL 168, 839–962.

115. Alain of Lille, *Elucidatio in cantica canticorum,* PL 210, 53B.

116. 8, 4; 70 *passim;* 73, 1 and 2; 75 *passim.*

117. 70, 1 and 2.

118. 7, 1.

119. 8, 4.

120. 54, 7; 56, 3.

121. 106, 9.

122. 8, 3.

123. 35, 1.

124. *Ibid.* 1

125. *Ibid.* 4

126. 8, 7. Robert Javelet, *Image et ressemblence au douzième siécle: de Saint Anselme à Alain de Lille;* tome 1 (1967) p. 89: 'Sans doute la créature, douée de raison, porte elle-même une certain image de Dieu; mais c'est tout autrement. Elle est créée; le Fils, *qui est né,* est l'Image consubstantielle, co-égale, co-éternelle, la seule véritable Image du Père.'

127. Javelet, *Ibid.,* pp. 72f.

128. 104, 3.

129. *Ibid.* 5.

130. 27, 4. 5.

131. 25, 6.

132. 27, 5.

133. 8, 3–5.

134. 26, 3; 61, 11; 109, 5.

135. 1, 4; 11, 1; 27, 8.

136. 49, 3; 59, 5.

137. 119, 1; 106, 1.

138. 109, 5.

139. Javelet, pp. 102–110.

140. 58, 13.

141. 5. 1.

142. 103, 5.

143. 36, 6.

144. 98, 5.

145. 9, 4; 14, 2; 109, 5; 110, 1.

146. 57, 13.

147. Appendix, 10.

148. 46, 8.

149. Javelet, pp. 108–110.

150. 21, 2.

151. 95, 10.

152. 102, incipit.

153. Javelet, p. 91.

154. 8, 4.

155. *Summa Theologiae,* pars tertia, 47, 3: '*Utrum Deus Pater tradiderit Christum passioni*'.

156. 10, 7.

157. 5, 1; 6, 8.

158. 82, 1.

159. 35, 1. 7.

160. This section is a summary of my article, 'The Idea of the Church in the Sermons of John of Ford,' *Cîteaux* 21 (1970) 236–264.

161. 14, 8.

162. 13, 2s.

163. 5, 2.

164. 56 and 57.

165. 57, 4.

166. 33, 7. Guerric of Igny expresses this same idea but puts rather more stress on personal salvation; see John Morson, *Christ the Way: The Christology of Guerric of Igny* (CS 25 forthcoming). Chapter III B, 'The Wounds of Christ'.

167. 30, 6.

168. 17, 9.

169. 59; 60.

170. 116, 2; cf 90, 1.

171. For example: 6, 2–4; 50, 6–7.

172. This aspect of the Church is especially prominent in the later sermons: namely, 112; 113; 115; 116.

173. 17, 9; 66, 10.

174. 6, 2.

175. 78, 3. John is probably thinking of the passage by St Gregory the Great, *Moralia,* book 1, ch. 14 (PL 75, 535CD). But if he is, he has given it a slightly different order.

176. 110, 2.

177. 54, 7–9.

178. 67, 10.

179. 29, 2; 32, 2.

180. Javelet, *Image et ressemblence* (see note 26).

181. 59, 8; cf 6, 2.

182. 101, 2; 77, 5.

183. 101, 5. 6.

184. 104, 3.

185. 104, 3.

186. 29, 2; 34, 2.

187. 4, 4; 108, 5.

188. 16, 3.

189. 4, *passim.*

190. 108, 5.

191. 74, 2.

192. St Bernard, *Tractatus de gradibus humilitatis et superbiae* 3, 6; OB 3:20, ll. 12–15, 'And now we can give this definition of humility: humility is the virtue by which a man comes to be despicable in his own eyes through the discovery and knowledge of what he is' (translation taken from *'The Steps of Humility'* by G. Webb and A. Walker; London: Mowbray Fleur de Lys Series, p. 22).

193. 73, 5.

194. 101, 1.

195. 73, 5.

196. 51, 7.

197. *Ibid.,* 1. 2.

198. 106, 12.

199. *Ibid.,*

200. 103, 6.

201. *Ibid.,* 8.

202. 106, 6.

203. 65, 1–2.

204. *Ibid.,* 4.

205. 37, 2.

206. *Ibid.,* 3. 5.

207. 4, 6–7; 82, 8.

208. 15, 7-8; 22, 3-5; 30, 2-4. 6; 53, 1-6; 91, 9-10; 119, 5-6.

209. 22, 4: ' . . . *ut scholam arcanae philosophiae istius ingrediatur* . . . ' (Reading *philosophiae* instead of *prophetiae* which is a mistake).

210. *Ibid.,* 6.

211. 53, 5.

212. 56, 3; 93, 6; 97, 1. Cf. 2, 3.

213. 22, 5; 76, 5.

214. 75, 1; 78, 5.

215. 17, 8.

216. 100, 2.

217. 79, 3.; 115, 11.

218. 108, 5; 104, 12.

219. 79, 2.

220. 8, 7. 8.

221. 12, 4; 14, 3.

222. For example: 58, 4; 72, 7.

223. 56, 9; 43, 10.

224. 110, 11.

225. 7, 3; 56, 9; 68, 3.

226. 100, 8.

227. Hilary Costello, 'John of Ford and the Quest for Wisdom', *Cîteaux* 23 (1972) p. 141–159.

228. 13, 1.

229. 52, 9.

230. 53, 1.

231. 114, 6.

232. 46, 8; 1 Co 6:17.

233. 97, 8: 'And so the soul, thirsting after the fountain of life, is by God's assistance trapped and held fast in a most powerful bond of loving desire. She is held fast and held tight, and in this tight hold she is drawn away from exterior things and drawn towards interior things in all their blissfulness. Sweetly she is drawn, and through love she clings to Christ. Joyfully she clings and is wedded to him and made with him one spirit'.

234. 111, 7.

235. *Ibid.* 8.

236. 68, 2.

237. 65, 9.

238. 97, 4.

239. Richard of St Victor, *Selected Writings on Contemplation;* Translated by Clare Kirchberger (London, 1957) *Benjamin Major,* ch. 4, p. 138 (PL 196, 67D). Cf 108, 8. 9.

240. 94, 3.

241. 16, 2; 47, 4.

242. 16, 2.

243. 24, 4.

244. 34, 7; 47, 7; 94, 2.

245. 18, 1.

246. 16, 2. Cf *D Sp*, art.: '*Imitation du Christ*', t. 7, col. 1571-3.

247. 18, 2.

248. *Ibid.* 2.

249. 4, 1; 32, 2; 107, 7; 112, 9.

250. 20, 1.

251. 45, 5.

252. *Ibid.*

253. 114, 4. 5.

254. 118, 1.

255. 114, 10.

256. 62, 11.

257. 71, 7.

258. 104, 3; 28, 2.

259. 108, 7.

260. 75, 4.

261. 71, 7.

262. 68, 8.

263. 55, 8.

264. 2, 1. 2; 7, 1.

265. 26, 5; 7, 2.

266. 54, 2. 4.

267. *Ibid.* 2–4.

268. 85, 130–134: 'It has thrown out roots far and wide into the towns, castles and villages of France, and its branches have spread out over Italy. Alas! the Princes of these areas have been infected with its cankerous growth. There seems little or no hope of rooting out this vile seed.'

# TRANSLATOR'S PREFACE

MANY A TRANSLATOR (though perhaps not in the Cistercian Fathers Series) is faced with the delicate task of explaining why, with several translations of his author already current, he should feel it incumbent on himself to offer a new one. Of this embarrassment I am happily free: John of Ford's Sermons have not been translated before, though I cannot but feel, with mingled humiliation and hope, that they are certain to be translated again! There is no mystery about this. To the best of our present knowledge, only one manuscript is extant, preserved for posterity by Balliol College, Oxford. The real mystery, of course, is why there should only be this one manuscript. In his relative youth, John produced a life of Wulfric of Haslebury, a saintly anchorite living near the abbey, and this juvenilium was a great success, much transcribed and hence still available in a good many manuscript collections. It is difficult to understand why the work of his maturity should, apparently, have fallen so completely flat. One is tempted to idle speculation, to wonder if the Interdict was to blame, or even if John's short term as King John's confessor had involved him in the unpopularity of that most detested of monarchs. All scholarship can suggest is that the thirteenth century had rather lost interest in the Canticle sermon, which seems almost like saying that the declining vogue of the murder story will also empty our shelves of, say, *The Brothers Karamazov.* John is larger than his medium, as Doestoyevsky, that greater artist, is of his.

Whatever the attitude of the thirteenth century, we can be in no doubt as to that of the twentieth. Sermons are not our favorite art form. They are still published—we need only think of *The True Wilderness* and the revealing critical applause for Williams' brilliance in giving each sermon the impact of a short story—but with no editorial expectations of best-seller status. It is not that our age is uninterested in the fundamentals of life and death, few have been more, but the shape our preoccupations create for themselves is not that of the sermon, but of the novel. In her masterly introduction to the *Purgatorio,* Dorothy L. Sayers speaks of the allegorical poem being for the fourteenth century what the novel is for ours, 'the dominant literary form, into which a writer could pour, without incongruity, everything he had to say about life and the universe.'* Every age has this 'dominant form,' and one may feel, too, that every age uses it to say much the same thing. To put it concretely, *The Lord of the Flies, Requiem for a Nun,* and *The Golden Bowl* are basically concerned with issues that preoccupied Augustine, Bernard and the other great medieval writers, but in a form so different as almost to be transmuted out of recognition. Anyone who has experienced the full impact of Chaucer will remember the exhilerating shock of finding oneself taken into a new universe. All is the same, and yet the emphases are not our own, the implicit assumptions are different, there is a fresh hierarchy of values. When, at the end of *Troylus and Cresseyda,* Troylus is killed amid a welter of disillusion and heartbreak, his dead self looks down on the world, on Troy, the battlefield,

*The Comedy of Dante Alighieri the Florentine: Cantica II, Purgatory,* tr. Dorothy L. Sayers (Penguin Books, 1955) p. 14.

and his own body. He looks down, and laughs. Anyone who can enter into the supreme rightness of the laughing Troylus, will be able to appreciate both the difference and the sameness of John of Ford.

This subtle and fascinating combination, familiar matter both concealed and revealed by the unfamiliarity of the expression, poses a peculiar problem for the translator. Obviously the ideal is to present one's author in the language of the present, to lend him, as far as possible, one's own tongue to speak with. Yet, paradoxically, the imaginative leap always required to enter into a world that is past may seem fatally unimportant if the past becomes too 'present.' It is somehow easier to understand Castiglione's *Courtier* in its original Renaissance translation than in its modern. Even more strikingly, the 'modernization' of Julian of Norwich (where, for example, 'Yea, dear Lord, gramercy!' appears, no doubt correctly, as 'Yes, Lord, thank you very much') has the unexpected effect of distancing her. The attempt to make her speak as we do only emphasises the fact that she did not think as we do, that a woman of today would say it all quite differently. I found myself, therefore, in a real dilemma. The more relevant I could make John's manner, the more smooth and flowing and idiomatic the style, the more danger I faced that his matter might seem irrelevant and the true depths of his thought be unappreciated. On the other hand, deliberately to embark on a pastiche of pre-Chaucerian English seemed to countervene every canon of the translator's craft. There is no solution, but since one must do one or the other, I have taken as a guide-line that 'the end does not justify the means.' To write a false language would be untrue, to John as well as to myself. It would also be very difficult, but that is by the way! I have consequently done my very best to give John an acceptable modern dress, and its inadequacies are due solely to inadvertance and ineptitude. I can only implore the reader to make the effort necessary to meet this wise and holy writer, and to believe that, though not a man of our time, he is very much a man for our time. When his thought seems strange, this is nearly always an occasion to explore its riches. When his expression seems strange, it is nearly always an occasion to deplore a poor translation.

This all-too-noticeable gap between ideal and performance would be even more distressing had it not been for the ungrudging assistance of Father Hilary Costello, writer of the introduction to the present volume and joint editor with Father Edmund Mikkers of the Balliol mss. Not only has he polished up the style, but he has contrived to keep me from many a misunderstanding or half-appreciation of a nuance. He contrived this, moreover, without once failing in tact, but even had he trampled on the tenderest feelings, my debt would be immense. I would also like to thank Father Basil Pennington, and Doctor Rozanne Elder, a patient and considerate editor-in-chief, and last but not least, Dom Ambrose Southey, Abbot General of the Cistercians of the Strict Observance and formerly Abbot of Mount Saint Bernard, through whose kindness John of Ford's Sermons came to be entrusted to my grateful if graceless hands.

*W. M. B.*

*Quidenham*
*Easter, 1973*

# SERMON ON THE SONG OF SONGS, I

*TEXT*

HERE BEGINS THE PROLOGUE OF DOM JOHN, THE VENERABLE ABBOT OF FORD, TO HIS SERMONS ON THE LATTER PART OF THE SONG OF SOLOMON, FROM THE WORDS OF 'MY BELOVED IS ALL RADIANT AND RUDDY' TO THE END.

I F ANYONE THINKS I SHOULD BE CENSURED for rashness and pride in not fearing to set my hand to the sacred mysteries of divine love, where the holy angels themselves must fall prostrate in adoration, I shall not be surprised! Who, after all, am I not to have been seized with dread at putting my shoulders under a weight so huge and plunging into the waters? These are waters in which even the elephants[1] have swum, and the giants themselves have groaned within the depths.* I must feel apprehension that I disfigured so superlative a theme with my thoughts and words, so that those who read and hear such a botched piece of work will say in mockery: This man began to build and was not able to finish.*

2. Lord Jesus, this is your business. You must take up its defence on my behalf! You know, most loving Jesus, that

[1] *The reference is to the authors John used as sources, e.g. Origen, St Bernard, Gilbert of Hoyland, Richard of St Victor.*

*Jb 26:5

*Lk 14:30

it was because of desire for your love that
I over-reached myself. Support me with
your hand in case I fall, and speak out on
my behalf so that I do not sink beneath
my false accusers. Redeem me from the
*Ps 119:34*  false accusations of men,* if it happens
that anyone should set himself to oppose
this holy theme. Do not let me be overwhelmed by a groundless distrust, but
rather turn away from me the reproach
*Ps 119:39*  which I dread.* Most tranquil, most gentle,
most wise of Lords, set in motion, regulate
and direct in your servant's hands this
pen, the obedient servant of your love! At
your good pleasure, steep it in the ink of
your spirit. For to you, most beautiful
among the sons of men, into your power,
has the Father given the ink of writers, so
that from your ink into our little vessels
you may pour according to the measure of
*Ep 4:7*  your giving.* If in my presumption I have
made a fool of myself, give me strength!
May the boldness of this confidence win a
place of pardon before you, for it is solely
on your goodness that I presume! What
would be an adequate excuse in this matter
but charity alone? And it is charity that
I have undertaken to serve in this work to
the praise of your holy name. Burning with
the desire of your love, I said to myself in
thought: Who will give me of the fountain
of the living waters of my Lord,* so that I
*Jr 17:13*  may drink and be inebriated and forget
my wretchedness? Who will give me to run
to his embrace, whom every creature in
heaven and earth testifies is lovable? Who

will intimate something of the art of loving? Who will set down the first principles? Who will provide a rule? And all of a sudden, while I was thrashing this out with my soul, the thought came to me of the song of your love, your holy nuptial canticle in all its sweetness.

3. At the beginning of this song I find your bride—that soul, whoever it is, whom you deign to call by this glorious title—I find her yearning and sighing most ardently that she may deserve to enjoy the kiss of your most sacred mouth. Straightaway I hear your consoling words to her, in which you gladly bestow on this bride of yours the kindest looks and the sweetest speech. Here the proffered joys of your consolation are sometimes bestowed upon the daughters of Jerusalem, joys which come to them as it were like little sips of that delight, imparted by your bride. It was in rivalry of them that there was enkindled within me a bold wild eagerness of longing, so that through their example, I might dare, Lord, to desire the desire of your love, so desirable and lovable. Seeing how helpless I am, how wretched, it is too great a thing, o Spouse of my lady, that I should sigh after the delights of my Lord, and so I have resolved, by your favor, to pass for a time into the portion and number of the maidens, a number past counting.* I have learned from your teaching, good master, when I am invited to a wedding feast, to choose for myself the lowest place,* so that I can go up higher when you visit me.

*Ps 104:25

*Lk 14:8

*Sg 1:3*

Accordingly, it is my ardent intention and as it were my duty, under your inspiration, to draw my brothers and fellow servants to the odor of your ointments,* o Lord my God. My good intentions will themselves serve towards their advancement, seeing that it was your pleasure to set me aside as their servant. In fear and trembling I am already mindful of that day, soon to come, when you must demand an account of my stewardship and I must render it. If you examine suddenly and too strictly, Lord, who could abide it?* What of the pasturing of your sheep, which in a threefold injunction of the prince of shepherds you laid in your love on all shepherds, once, twice, and again: what am I to reply to you when you ask me about this? Woe to me on that day if the land,[2] which you entrusted to me for cultivation, has cried out against me, and its furrows have wept together!* Therefore, in slight mitigation of my burden and payment of my debt, I have taken care to forestall your presence, o Lord, my judge, and to apply myself to feeding your flock by timely encouragement. But o, greatest of shepherds, by that deathless love of yours, which made you leave on the mountains all your own, (the angels), and come to seek us, your lost sheep,[3] do not, I beg and entreat you, yourself neglect to feed those whose pasturing you have committed to me! Do not, I implore, let your finding of them be in vain, do not let my sloth lose again what your love has found! It will be

*Ps 130:3*

[2] For tertia *read* terra *as in the MS.*

*Jb 31:38*

[3] *An allusion to the patristic interpretation of Mt 18:12–13 and also Mt 19:27, that Christ left the angels in heaven (on the mountains) to save us, his lost sheep.*

my duty, through your gift, to serve at the gates, but yours to work within, you who teach men wisdom,* touching the heart with spiritual unction. The task you have given me will be to display in speech or writing some of the significance of your words, but it is your task, by the finger of God which is the Holy Spirit, to write deep in the soul what these words mean.

*Ps 94:10

4. Furthermore, with reference to the merits of those who have set their hand to this song,[4] no one need stir up ill feeling because of my insignificance, no one need exert himself in being abusive about knowledge and eloquence! These men have nothing which was not given them from heaven. Their glory is not lessened by my paltry effort, on the contrary, it grows greater by comparison. In all truth I acknowledge that this offering, which I have put into the treasury,* is paltry indeed, but the eye of Jesus, that kindly eye, in its loving appraisal is wont to add weight to the paltry. If I emulate them, it is with a divine emulation,* not in rivalry; in humility, not stubbornness; in a reverent imitation and not an arrogant competition! Let me say, then, that I have the greatest desire to hasten after that famous man, and I refer to blessed Bernard, not envious of his glory, but trailing in his footsteps. I am not boldly running to catch up but trying in all humility to follow after him, not striving to keep pace with the giant but striding out as best I can, not strolling along at his side but reverencing the

[4] *John was one of a succession of writers on the Song of Solomon, by far the greatest of whom was St Bernard.*

*Mk 12:43

*Cf 2 Co 11:2

footprints that ever stretch ahead of me. May that most eminent man, whose glory is to have expounded the Song of Songs, enjoy the full prerogative of his achievement! Through the spirit of wisdom he merited to speak more beautifully than others of what he had so uniquely experienced through the spirit of charity.

And now, my brothers, my masters, you will console your servant not a little if you take with cheerfulness what has been prepared for you. In the sweat of my brow I have reaped and threshed, I have ground and baked this bread for you. I shall think the work well repaid if you do not scorn eating of it. To be sure, the well is deep,* as you can see for yourselves, from which I have been intent on drawing water for you to drink. And since the flask of my mind is rather meagre, the drawing had to be fairly frequent, and my hand is inexpert at the work. And so, here is your water! Taste it, and if it tastes good, you have refreshed my soul. But if, on the contrary, your first reaction is to find it tasteless, see if perhaps this is not rather the fault of your palate than of the draught. Still, whatever the reason, whether the fault is on one side or perhaps on both, the Lord is close at hand,* and by his blessing he can transform the lost taste of water and to heal the jaded relish of the palate.

5. For the rest, seeing that in much speaking sin is not easily avoided,* if any mistake has crept into my writing, and too much ink—or too little—has flowed from

*Jn 4:11

*Is 55:6

*Pr 10:19

my hastening pen, I humbly beg the kind reader to forgive it. Nevertheless, what I have just said does not apply to the truth of faith. On that, whoever loves Christ will not accept calmly anything in the slightest degree injurious. If the reader finds any mistake in this area, I entreat him to wield his lancet without mercy. Let me not be judged without mercy, however, because my wish is not to persist in my error but instantly to retract it.

6. As I searched deep into the furthest nooks and crannies of my heart, a threefold purpose suggested itself. First and foremost, that I might offer the Lord God my savior the service of my lips as a sacrifice of praise. Secondly, to serve fraternal charity and to discharge to some small degree the debt which I acknowledge I owe my brothers. Thirdly, that my own soul might catch fire from these words of burning eloquence, now that they have come within my hands. For those who work in the kitchen, there is fire close at hand to keep them warm, and so for me, your servant, working among the words of the Holy Spirit, the numbness which chills me may grow less troublesome. To drive away this vexatious numbness, or at least lessen it, it seemed to me that nothing could be more effective than the fire at which, in this nuptial song, the bride of the Lord does not restrain her soul from fainting and melting away.

I have no doubt that to the fastidious ear the length of this work will seem annoying, and for this I beg the reader's pardon, though at this stage, remorse comes rather late! To be honest, I took pains to avoid brevity, on the grounds that to the simpler mind it is less impressive, and far from unfolding elevated sentiments as their majesty demands, it rolls them up and crushes them into a verbal strait-jacket. Still, intent on what was simpler and easier, my rejection of the steep and narrow shortcut has forced me to undertake the labor of a longer journey. By way of lightening the burden and relieving the tedium, however, there is this remedy: if you want to run quickly through the sermons, you will find a short summary of the contents attached to each one—a summary not provided for the whole work.

7. *To you, Lord Jesus, I entrust this work of mine in its entirety. I entreat you, as the faithful guardian of my trust, not to blot out of the book of life this thing that I have taken such pains over, to give you honor. Grant, too, that from this little sowing I may reap some fruit of edification for my brothers. You, o God, the strength of my heart and my portion for ever,\* who now deign to be seed in the hand of the sower, be on that day, I pray, a sheaf in the hand of the reaper! For you are the end and beginning of every good work, the aim and reward, the glory and blessing of your faithful people, spouse of the church, praise of the angels, power and wisdom of God the Father, who with the same Father and the Holy Spirit,*

\*Ps 73:25

*lives and reigns, God,*
*for ever and ever.*
*Amen.*


HERE ENDS THE PROLOGUE

# SERMON ONE

*These are the paragraph headings of the first sermon:* With what care and in what places the bride is wont to seek her spouse, and how, when she does not find him, she grows languid. With what great fervor of desire the activity of 'adjuring' is to be understood, so that her langor may be told to her beloved. Why she speaks rather of langor than of illness. How humbly she presumes that he whom she herself has not found, will have been found by others. How prudently, under the cloak of her own need, she sees to the wellbeing of her subjects and brothers.

*Here begins the first sermon.*

I ADJURE YOU, o daughters of Jerusalem, if you find my beloved, that you tell him I languish with love.* Charity, poured forth into the bride's heart as a pledge that her spouse has graciously taken the initiative and endowed her more richly than other mortals, works upon her with great power. Its actions vary, not always influenced by the same emotions, for at first love conceives, with much sweetness of spirit, what it will afterwards bring to earth with painful labor. In the

*Sg 5:8

77

beginning there are kisses, there are endearments—treasure chambers are displayed, face is displayed to face, the left hand is under the head and the right hand devoted to holy embrace.* Who would doubt at this point that the bride has come to the full realization of her desires and has not been disappointed of what she craved?* But spiritual delights, once experienced, cause unease, and though they satisfy at the time, in the long run they afflict. Kisses once enjoyed are eagerly sought again, and the more richly the abundance of her spouse satisfied the bride's desires in the past, the more bitterly are those favors mourned when they are over. The beloved is sought and not found; he is called and he does not answer.

The bride endures all this because charity endures all things,* and consoles herself as best she can with the bare memory of her beloved. For putting all else completely out of mind and, as it were, burying it in deep forgetfulness, while the bridegroom delays,* while the king is on his couch,† she strains with fragrant sighs and ardent longing to draw him from the bosom of the Father. And so the spouse delays and the bride makes progress in love. He delays the joys of his chosen one, but this delay, as the bride recognizes is for her good. In the meantime, he looks searchingly at her from behind his eyelids,* and, in the way of ardent lovers, uses his very absence to test the fidelity of her love, according to the words, The Lord our God is testing you, to

*Cf. Sg 2:6

*Ps 78:30

*1 Co 13:7

*Mt 26:5
*Sg 1:12

*Cf. Ps 11:5

know if you love him or not.* What heavier
trial for a soul seeking God, than to be
kept from finding him? As there is no
joy like the joy he gives, so, if I dare say it,
is there no sorrow like the sorrow he gives.
As are his delights, so are the exhaustion
and weariness, the langor and misery he
causes.

2. She hurries back to the places that
witnessed their secret meetings and were
hallowed by chaste pleasure. She enters
her bedchamber. She shuts out everything
that could offend the eyes of her spouse or
disturb his enjoyment, and she does not
forget the bolt of her door, in case, according to his custom, the doors being shut,
Jesus may wish to enter.* Furthermore,
even the time most apt for lovers is eagerly
seized upon, since the spouse is wont to
appear while all things are in silence in the
middle of the night.* It is at midnight that
the Bride is accustomed to hear: 'Behold,
the bridegroom comes!'* The secret and
hidden lover of Jesus makes darkness his
hiding place,* and when sleep customarily
takes hold of men, it seems, he gives himself more utterly to the embraces of his
beloved. Therefore, expecting to enjoy
her beloved as she had yesterday and the
day before, she composes herself gracefully
on her bed, relying on the assistance of
seemly place and hour. She spreads wide
her arms, she opens out her heart, she
pours forth her soul, in spiritual longing she
draws to herself the breath of his love.
Anxious and wakeful she keeps vigil the

*Dt 13:3*

*Jn 20:26*

*Cf. Ws 18:14*

*Mt 25:6*

*Ps 18:11*

*Lk 5:5

whole night; yet laboring all night,* she catches nothing, and after all her watching is wretchedly disappointed and confounded in her hopes.

3. Jesus is absent, he is not here. Only loneliness and desolation dwell in chamber and in bed. She considers everything in her possession petty, and becoming oppressive to herself she bursts forth from her inner room in distress of mind. She goes out into the streets and lanes of the city, because wisdom, as she well knows, cries aloud in the street, raises her voice in the markets.* Perhaps, also, in imitation of her spouse, since the person who says he abides in him ought to walk in the way he walked,* she wishes in her turn to spread his streams abroad and to distribute his waters to the streets.* For she knows that Jesus draws near to those who speak of him, and that in the breaking of bread, which is the Word of God, he commonly reveals the face of his glory.* A liberal man will be enriched, and one who waters will himself be watered.*

So, steadily pursuing her aim, the bride goes out swiftly into the streets and lanes. She presses eagerly through the streets, persistently through the lanes, sharing the word of love with each man according to his capacity. Among the mature she imparts wisdom,* and she feeds the weak, not with solid food, but with milk.* She has, in fact, breasts swollen with milk, and she is quite ready to become a nurse even to little ones, as long as they belong to the Lord. She calls all those whom she finds

*Pr 1:20

*Cf. 1 Jn 2:6

*Pr 5:16

*Cf. Lk 24:35
*Pr 11:25

*1 Co 2:6
*1 Co 3:2

walking the paths of life in the streets and
lanes of Jerusalem, and begs and implores
them in the Lord Jesus that, as they have
begun to walk, so they go on walking until
they arrive. If, in a market place so filled
with great and precious bargains, she finds
anyone idle, she vigorously rouses and urges
him on, for he reckons such precious
merchandise worthless. Rather, he does
not appreciate that in this life these things
are both precious and cheap together, and
can be bought at such a low price. But the
spouse does not yet come to meet the
ardently pursuing bride. As some kind of
solace, however, there do come to meet
her the watchmen of the city, of whom she
can meanwhile inquire. For sometimes the
Lord Jesus is accustomed to reveal his richness more readily to those who inquire
about him then to those who dispute about
him. To reward listening more copiously
than speaking is his way, and often those
are accounted more blessed who hear the
word of God than those who proclaim it.*          *Lk 11:28*

To resume then: the beloved of the
Lord Jesus, whose sole need is to seek him
whom her soul loves, seeks him before all
else on the couch of secret and assiduous
meditation, and she does not find him. She
sets herself to find him in the exercise of
holy preaching, and there, too, she is not
rewarded by finding him. Finally, she
betakes herself to the third kind of seeking,
namely, that of humble listening in silence.
On her bed, within doors, she reposes in her
own company. Out of doors, in the streets,

she discusses in the company of others. In
the presence of the guards she is both
indoors and out, for in asking questions she
goes out and in hearing she retreats within.
In short, observing all the ways of the
Lord Jesus with the utmost care, and
following them closely, first she seeks him
in the chamber of inner peace. Then she
hastens forth in the service of brotherly
edification. Last of all, she comes down
from the teacher's chair to the humble
position of a pupil that she may ask about
her beloved; perhaps in this place Jesus
may regard the lowliness of his handmaid.*

*\*Lk 1:48*

Now he refrains no longer from raising
up the soul of his beloved, exhausted and
languid with excessive fatigue. He fulfills
the desire of all who fear him*—how much
more of those who love him, and love him
so much! Hope does not disappoint,*
especially when charity pours itself forth.
And so, at the plea of his loved one, her
desired appears. He steals into her arms,
there to be clasped all the more closely,
enjoyed all the more sweetly, held all the
more strongly, because the search was so
long, the pursuit so difficult, the finding so
long delayed. The bride reaps with full
hands the fruits of her labors, and rejoices
in them like one who finds great spoil,* as
men rejoice with joy at the harvest.* She
possesses her beloved, and that is enough
for her. She asked one thing, she sought
and pursued it, and this she has found.
Blessed in attaining her desire, she has in
turn but one anxiety, that she may hold

*\*Ps 145:19*

*\*Rm 5:5*

*\*Ps 119:162*
*\*Is 9:3*

what she holds, and that he who is held
may not slip away. All the rejoicing of
lovers finds expression in their mutual fond
exchanges, and words sweeter than honey
flow from his honeysweet lips. Admiring
compliments are offered and returned, as
full of real sincerity as of secret consolation, and from the endearments that come
tenderly to a lover's ears, charity takes fire
and flares up like oil on the flames.

4. What more can I say? The keen
arrows of love fly so thickly, they strike
with such quivering force, that not only
does the spouse confess that his heart has
been wounded by the bride, but she too,
no less languid with love, adjures the
daughters of Jerusalem at her side to let the
bridegroom know her langor. Indeed, only
he who caused the wound can supply the
remedy. He has deigned to stretch out his
healing hand to other wounds, so why
should he not show his power over a wound
so loving, a pain so salutary, a weakness so
strong, a langor so extraordinary? Furthermore, if it is the gift of infinite grace that
the bride is privileged to languish with such
a blessed sickness, how much more should
she look to that same grace for the spouse
to bear help to his beloved on her bed of
pain! Finally, if the Lord Jesus explains his
name as meaning the salvation of all, how
much more it behooves him to save his
chosen one in her great need, unfolding
fully the power of his title!

Confident of this, she sends him an embassy herself, not burdening them with

many words or impressing upon them more than this one thing, that they tell her beloved that she languishes with love. For so powerful a healer, it is enough to be told the disease and its nature. It is enough to have shared with so dear a friend the mere fact of sickness, without also begging for health. In days gone by, when Martha and Mary saw that death was threatening their brother Lazarus, they sent Jesus the message: 'Lord, he whom you love is sick,'* quite content with a brief mention of his friend's langor. When the wine failed at the marriage feast, the mother of Jesus said to her Lord and Son in the same brief way: 'They have no wine.'* She obviously believed that to have mentioned the matter was all that was needed. She spoke of the lack, and meanwhile refrained from petition, unless, indeed, the desire of that heart, so worthy of reverence, sounded more loudly in his ears than any petition. All desire, above all one so holy, is very eloquent. So the bride of the Word of God believes that when she is with her almighty spouse she has no need at all of busying herself with the exigencies of petition. She is in his possession, and the most powerful reason for being cured is that she is somebody who languishes for his love.

5. Observe, though, that she does not say that she is sick with love or ill with love, but that she languishes with love. She seems to be trying to indicate a state of weakness not easily cured. He is keeping away so that such sweet and holy love may

*Jn 11:3

*Jn 2:3

remain untouched by any kind of trivial remedy or, like other ills, look forward to being healed by a change of season or the passage of time. The wound of the beloved, who refuses all consolation under heaven and shuns relief, is incurable by preference. I think she would like the daughters of Jerusalem to languish with the same illness. It is not with devout entreaty, as is customary, nor with the force of a rather pressing order that she calls them to serve as this embassy, but she binds them solemnly under sacred oath. She truly pours forth on them the maternal solicitude with which she herself overflows. Imparting without grudging,* even more, persistently forcing her beloved upon them, she longs eagerly for them to share in her fullness. Of course, she wants all men to be saved,* but above all she desires that those for whom she is duty-bound to make provision should be as she herself is.

*Wis 7:13

*1 Tm 2:4

6.  Yet look well at the bride's humility. She feels fully confident that the beloved who has gone from her will have been found by the daughters of Jerusalem. She makes her happiness depend on this: that the joy denied her for a time is being offered to her daughters. Perhaps these are the remedies which she asked for in the past, when she acknowledged before them her langor in the words: 'Stay me with raisins, comfort me with apples, for I languish with love.'* Certainly the greatest comfort of souls all on fire and languishing with love is to be able to set others alight

*Sg 2:5

with the same fire and wound them with a like hurt.

7.   These trees of paradise, trees wholly fragrant, contain within themselves the seed of their kind, so that from them trees of the same nature may grow and multiply.* *Cf. Gn 1:11-12 If you remember, you have some examples of this kind of charity in Sara and Rachel. Because they themselves could not conceive they offered their handmaids to their husbands as a consolation for their own infertility, and they shared their husbands with their handmaids, regarding as born to themselves what came of this. This is a goodness well worth fostering and imitating—one which makes both the joys and fruits of another its own, for it considers them as such. Yet these images, as I said, were but examples. The sacred reality you can behold more clearly in the bride of the Word of God. For, seeing them hastening to enter the bliss of her own condition, she adjures the daughters of Jerusalem to waste no time in imitating the ardor of this love. It is a love to be longed for and desired above everything else, [a love] which makes her suffer and burn and languish. Then they, too, will run to the embrace of the Word of God, they, too, will sigh for the kiss of Christ Jesus. There is to be no objecting that the way is long and hard, no saying with Moses, 'Send some other man, I pray you,'* no hiding behind the cover of any excuse whatever. At the very beginning of that holy task, the power of her pointed adjuration has sheared away all

*\*Cf. Gn 1:11-12* (margin note)

*\*Ex 4:13* (margin note)

possible delay or subterfuge.

Be attentive, daughters of Jerusalem, run forward. Do not delay, I beg you, but tell the spouse that his chosen languishes for love. You are bearers of good news to the spouse, with these words you will easily come very close to the Word of God,
our Lord Jesus Christ,
who with the Father
and the Holy Spirit,
lives and reigns, one God,
for ever and ever.
Amen.

## SERMON TWO

*These are the paragraph headings of the second sermon.* That, when the daughters of Jerusalem are adjured to seek out the beloved, they carefully consider the charity of the bride, which makes her concerned about their progress. They seek him, indeed, but only in her presence, for she is his nuptial chamber. Wherefore they soon question her about the beauty of the spouse, seeing how it inflames the bride with his love.

WHAT IS YOUR BELOVED more than another beloved, o fairest among women?* When the daughters of Jerusalem are adjured by the Lord's bride to carry to her spouse words of tenderness, they do not refuse the responsibility of the charge laid upon them. Yet they are not unaware how great a thing it is for them to become intermediaries between such lovers, to be promoters of so sacred a covenant. Because they have long been nourished by the bride's words, and from long talks with her have learned what she personally desires from this service of theirs, they take it very much to heart. They consider that the

*Sg 5:9

89

matter of their salvation should be discussed in depth by their mother. They are fully aware that they are being sent to their beloved that they may learn to seek his face and never weary in the search and never stop till they have found him. They are being sent to the spouse as if already weaned by the bride and able to accept some favor more solid from the table of the Father of lights. They are being sent so that from now on they may be accustomed to the sight of his glory. Up to now they have been used to seeing the glory of the spouse in the face of the bride, and they have been wonderfully illumined by her as from some everlasting mountain.* Now the time has come for them to contemplate with the apostles the glory of the Lord with face unveiled, and in light itself to see light.* The matter at issue, under the bride's fostering care, is the passing out of the pleasing state of maidenhood to receive a more sacred and significant title. A new name is to be given them, one which the mouth of the Lord has uttered, and from being maidens they will rise to being queens.

So it is that, without vulgar ostentation but with the most courteous kindness and the humblest charity, the bride shares all with her daughters, all the goodly blessings with which her spouse has met her,* whether the sighing of a holy kiss or the fragrance of the choicest perfumes or the very secrets of the marriage bed, the most glorious of honors. Surely this is her motive, not alone to arrive at these blessings

*Cf. Ps 76:4

*Cf. Ps 36:9

*Ps 21:3

but, as we have read, to have her virgin companions led after her to the king.* It *Ps 45:15 was in this spirit, I think, that John sent his disciples to Jesus. If he tore them from his breasts he could hand them over to a stronger meat and master, proving himself a faithful friend to the bridegroom, for whose bride he was so loyally zealous. And so the bride, whom a little earlier the spouse thought fit to call friend, by the deepest law of friendship hands over completely that most blessed part, which shall not be taken away from her.* She pours it *Lk 10:42 out into the bosom of the maidens in her train, even desiring to be surpassed by them in this holy warfare of love. Generally speaking, if the bride demands from the spouse anything just for herself, and looks for a personal glory, because she has been specially favored, she is sure to lose something of that glory of the bride whom the apostle describes as 'splendid, without spot or wrinkle or any such thing.'* The bride *Ep 5:27 has understood the spouse very differently, however, and given clear proof of it by desiring with an intense and universal impulse of charity that the name she inherits, a name splendid and distinguished above all others, should become their common property. In so doing, as has been already said more than once, she makes the maidens partners and messengers both in her ardor and in her langor, so that they, too, as does she, both burn and languish.

2. The daughters of Jerusalem, accepting the service laid on them, are anxious

to fulfil their task without the delay of
wandering after the troop of the beloved's
companions while trying to find him.
Hence their eagerness to be taught by the
bride about the beloved's appearance. 'What
is your beloved,' they ask, 'more than
another beloved, o fairest among women?'*
By this query about the beauty of the
spouse, they bring him sweetly to mind,
and by bringing him to mind they subtly
make the bride conscious of his presence.
They were sent to seek, and yet, in asking
the bride about his appearance, the search
has already started.

'What is your beloved?' they ask. You
have seen his beauty, to you alone among
mortals has that desirable face been shown.
It is impressed upon your senses, stamped
upon your inmost being. You are a queen:
teach your maidens! You are a mother: in-
struct your daughters! O fairest of women,
tell young and ignorant girls what your
beloved is like! We do not ask for the
moment who he is, what person, for we
know that he is no other than Jesus Christ,
the Word of God, the Son of the virgin. We
want rather to hear about loveliness and
graciousness, the outward signs of beauty.
Let curious searchers into truth, analysers
of greatness, who have no fear of being
overwhelmed by glory, no dread of bursting rudely into its presence, let them inquire about his nature and greatness. But
we follow the policy of the Samaritan
woman and keep the secret things that
need deep research for another age, that is

*Sg 5:9

to say, until the Messiah comes, he who is called Christ, who will show us all things.* *Jn 4:25* He has many things to tell us which now we cannot bear, because they are too weighty and we are too weak.* *Cf. Jn 16:12*

Humbly refraining, then, from grandeurs and marvels beyond us, we are content in the meantime† to be taught what your beloved is like, and taught, o fairest of women, from your own lips. For your voice is sweet,* we have your beloved's word for it, and your lips distill nectar.† The sweeter the love, the sweeter too the speech. Yes, your tongue is on fire and your speech is enkindled,* and we long for you to make our hearts glow again for your Jesus. We have the testimony of our dear Solomon: 'Precious treasure rests in the mouth of the wise'.* What is this 'precious treasure' if not your beloved, so totally desirable? And who is 'the wise' if not the one who has an intimate relish of Jesus, and whom Jesus relishes, too?† We are weary of these preachers of ours, preaching not so much Christ as themselves, and compounding the draught of truth for us in an impure vessel. Further, what they offer us they themselves do not wish to taste, and since they offer it in unclean vessels, we reject the offering when we see the vessels. Who would hesitate to spit out wine, even the purest, if he should see the one who tendered it spitting into it?

'But in your mouth, o beautiful one, praise is beautiful; honor befits you, o worthy of honor.* You are an overflowing

*†Interim—rich in meaning, with overtones of 'this present life', and 'until Christ comes in glory.'*

*Sg 2:15*

*†Sg 4:11*

*Ps 119:140*

*Pr 21:20*

*†Et quis sapiens, nisi qui sapit Iesum. et cui Iesus sapit?— this interplay of wisdom as a 'taste' or 'relish' was a favorite of Cistercian writers.*

*Si 15:9*

*Ps 23:5*
*Is 49:2*

cup, exceeding lovely.* You are a chosen
arrow of the Lord,* and you strike straight
to the heart, for it is from the heart you
are aimed. May the Word of the Lord be in
your hand! May your spouse come to us
from his bridal chamber, your heart, for if
we are to find him for you, it is first
necessary that you manifest him to us. To
make a careful search for him, what is more
certainly his dwelling place than you, o
fairest of women? You are his garden, his
bedchamber, his banqueting hall, his everything. If he has gone out, we shall wait for
him in your presence, for his return to you
will be most certain and most swift. Meanwhile, let it not vex you to break for your
hungry handmaids that bread of yours,

*Cf. Ws 6:20*

containing all flavor and sweetness.* Let
the heavenly manna of your wisdom flow
from your hands, and may your beloved
become sweet to us from your lips.'

3.  It should be observed, however, that
they do not simply say, 'What is your
beloved?', but they add the unusual words,
'What is your beloved more than another
beloved?', with reference to why he is dear
to you. For he has a certain majesty which
by right ought to be feared, he has a certain
kindliness which ought to be loved. We are
not inquiring from you about the terror of
his power, the depths of his designs, the
abyss of his judgments. These are the
domain of other preachers and perhaps of
other disciples. We ask of you a sweeter
and gentler nourishment. It is no effort for
you to speak of these things, and for us

it is a necessity. These riches are hidden deep within you. You have for your own possession, and you share with us at your pleasure, the knowledge of the charity of Christ, surpassing all knowledge.* You are the guardian and dispenser of goods so great; from your lips we seek that knowledge. It is theft and misuse if any foolish woman should wish to bedeck herself from your abundant treasure, applying to herself the symbolism that belongs to the beloved. 'Like a gold ring in a swine's snout,' says Solomon, 'is a beautiful woman without discretion'.* How long, o filthy swine, will you think you adorn yourself by taking the words of this sacred song into your unclean mouth? When you have bedecked yourself with a golden ring or a golden necklace or even golden ear-rings, your finery is wasted. Your mouth is not the place for wisdom, for fine speech is not becoming to a fool.* It is the bride's lips that protect wisdom, to her it is given to speak as she pleases. She is the one for whom the golden ring is fitting, also the golden necklace, the golden ear-rings, inlaid with silver, for she serves the cause of charity in all she does, thinks, hears; everything in her is directed towards charity. O fairest of women, all these emblems are yours. Anything that is made for adornment is the equipment of your beauty, the gear of your loveliness.

Loved one, speak about the beloved! Beauteous one, about the beautiful! Let your voice ring in the ears of your

*Cf. Ep 3:19

*Pr 11:22

*Pr 17:7

handmaids. 'What is your beloved more than another beloved, o fairest among women?' We hope indeed to have made some progress towards that beauty, for we cleave to your side, conformed to your desire, believing that from your words we have conceived the spirit of life and to some extent have already brought it forth. But our beauty, whatever it is, shows stained and wrinkled until the charity of your beloved is formed in us. It is from God's liberality and your efforts that we have drunk in or inhaled that spirit. Certainly we aspire to long after that love of Christ which has triumphed over you, and for the moment this is the small measure of our beauty. We shall not leave the shadow of your wings or our dependence on your breasts, sweeter than wine, until it is granted us from above to taste the better gifts and become worthy of the king's embrace. By gazing at your beauty, o most beautiful of women, we see clearly what we lack. Put forth your best endeavors, since you enjoy the favor of your beloved and your prayer cannot long go unanswered, that not only from your breasts but also in our own senses, we may know from now on what is your beloved, and our most
love-worthy, Jesus Christ, our Lord,
who with the Father and the Holy Spirit,
lives and reigns, one God,
for ever and ever.
Amen.

## SERMON THREE

*The beginning of the third sermon:* Of the fourfold radiance, that of milk, of lilies, of snow and of light, symbolizing four types of sanctity, that of children, of adults, of the penitent and of the resurrected.

**M**Y BELOVED IS ALL RADIANT and ruddy, distinguished among thousands.'* The bride of the Lord has been asked about her beloved, and to such godly desires she answers at once. She gladly discloses what she would freely have offered, even had she not been asked. A twofold charity draws her, for her beloved and for the daughters of Jerusalem. The charity of Christ is shown in that she so eagerly seizes the opportunity of declaring his praise, follows it up so fully, exploits it so willingly. But, with maternal affection, she serves no less the cause of those whom she fills with wonder and love by her ardent praise. Without any doubt, praise awakens love and preserves it. Hence it is that the citizens of Jerusalem feed the flame of eternal love by eternal praises. They cease not to cry aloud so as to be steadfast in love. Their cry has no rest, because love knows no intermission. So praise is the food of love. And you, too,

*Sg 5:10

if deep within you there is a little spark of
sacred love, do all you can to apply to this
spark the oil of your praise, so that your
tiny fire may live and grow. With this oil
you anoint Jesus, enriching charity. Love
waxes strong on praise, and, in turn, praise
is enkindled by love. Charity is dumb without praise, and praise, though it speak
with the tongue of angels,* is still mute
without charity.

*Cf. 1 Co 13:1*

So the mouth of the bride is open to the
daughters of Jerusalem, 'for her heart has
been enlarged.'* And who more apt for the
purpose? On this theme the bride of the
Lord is eloquent, to say the least! Certainly, out of the abundance of the heart
the mouth speaks.* The vessels of this
woman brim with oil, she comes to anoint
the whole Jesus. Let us therefore pay
attention to the lips of the bride. Perhaps
by the revelation of the Spirit it may be
granted us to comprehend a little of these
things which are beyond our own capacity.
But the Spirit of wisdom, to whose guidance
we entrust our words and their meanings,
is kindly.

*2 Co 6:11*

*Mt 12:34*

'My beloved,' she says, 'is all radiant and
ruddy, distinguished among thousands.'
This radiance, this redness, which the
bride admires in the face of her spouse, is
not just any kind of radiance or redness,
but, at the very least, a whiteness above all
other, a redness above all other. Leaving
aside for the moment the redness, let us, if
you will, compare that radiant whiteness to
those which our eye of flesh experiences.

2. There is the radiant whiteness of milk and the radiant whiteness of a lily, that of snow and that of light. You will find nothing, I think, in this visible creation that can be superior, perhaps nothing equal, to these in whiteness. But far be it from me to believe that any radiance of this sort is being praised in the spouse, especially by her whose eyes are as the eyes of doves,* and who has learned to gaze on her beloved spiritually. So if you, too, have known Christ, not according to the flesh but in the spirit,* you will assuredly see in him the whiteness of milk, of lilies, of snow and light. For there is an innocence of children and an innocence of adults, and again, there is an innocence which penitence restores and one which resurrection bestows at the last day.

*Sg 4:1

*Cf. 2 Co 5:16
*Cf. 2 Co 5:16

The first innocence is like milk. Milk is indisputably fitting for little ones, who by the twofold blessing of age and grace, keep joyfully and easily the innocence that came with them from their mother's womb and was sanctified in them by the waters of life. Blessed are they who, rising at dawn, complete the whole day's journey before the heat begins, carried in the arms of grace and free from all fear and danger. Blessed indeed are they whose mother, grace, brings them to perfection by so short a way, hiding her little ones from the sight of evil, drawing them away quickly lest they even glimpse wickedness. Blessed band, to whom it is given to triumph over so many enemies without a wound! The

prince of this world finds in them, I do not
say nothing but, very little.

The lamb of God is thronged about with
companions, closely conformed to him in
every way, so that even that period of
Christ's life may have those who play and
rejoice with him, who follow him where-
soever he goes.* Praise the Lord, you
children,† since you have rich matter for
praise! Lovely is the perfect praise and
graceful eulogy that sounds on your virgin
lips which no lie or stain of lust has defiled.
Out of the mouth of babes and sucklings
you have made perfect praise,* o my
Lord, Lamb of God, so that in the heavenly melody there may sound and resound
in your ears, as harmonious as sweet, the
tune of your little ones. Blessed race,
whiter than milk! You stand guiltless,
hence with utter confidence, before the
throne of God, having nothing to offend
the eyes of that judge, nothing to be
restored to pardon, but rather everything
which pleases and makes for grace. O
mother grace, with what clear proof you
show yourself to every conscience as desirable, these children of yours whom, without waiting for merit, you press forward
to the kingdom. You forestall in them all
deeds of evil, and you also forestall in
them all good. You claim them totally for
yourself, as [children] free from the stain
of sin through the blood of Christ, as
sharers in so great a glory through no effort
of their own. It is true that out of their
mouths you have made perfect praise, in

*Cf. Rev 4:4
†Ps 112:1

*Mt 21:16, Ps 8:3

order to confound your enemies, the foes of grace, who rely on their strength and merits, and so fall from grace, forsaken by merits both.

We see in the gospel, too, how when Jesus was talking about little children, he commanded the little ones to come to him, explained to them the kingdom of heaven, and then even tenderly embraced a little child himself.\* O how sweet a food *\*Cf. Mt 19:13* this was for little ones, what more than motherly affection! How greatness shrinks itself to the scale of children, or rather, how it pours itself forth and spreads itself wide! How he yearns over them, as a mother bird over her young! How moved he is for them, for when he had disclosed to them his kingdom, he enclosed them within it by his bodily embrace! O over-flowing graciousness, o rich store of sweet-ness! You direct the way of your little ones towards yourself, dear Jesus, as if you walked ahead of them. You admit them to partnership in the kingdom as if they were comrades. You set them "in the middle"\* *\*Mt 18:2* as a pattern to be followed, and you raise them to your bosom through sheer grace. You are in a true sense that good shepherd who carries his lambs in his arms and lifts them to his bosom.\* How great are these *\*Is 40:11* little ones thus magnified by you! Yes, they were small and weak in their own eyes, and this is enough to make them very great in yours. They were poor in their own merits, but very rich in your approval! It suffices them for all merit to have found with you. And this is what may be said about the whiteness of milk, that is, the innocence of little children.

3. But there is another whiteness, more radiant still. It is [the whiteness] of those who have dedicated themselves to chastity even from their youth, who have called purity their mistress. Amidst unwholesome deeds and words, as gracefully and wonderfully as a lily among thorns,* they budded forth an inviolable purpose. In the full heat of the fire, by an astounding miracle, they were not burnt, but they emerged from the fiery furnace for all to see, not only unhurt, but more than ever radiant in whiteness. Yes, indeed, the king of Babylon who lit the furnace, drew back, bewildered and stunned at such a thing happening. His valor and strength, which till then he had founded on loins and navel, did not help him on the day of battle, did not harm them.* Into the furnace of itching youth he threw quantities of the pitch of seductive example, he added the soft fat of pleasing appearance and flattering blandishments, and then he threw on fire darts—in other words, a convenient time and a place all ready to hand. The flame roared and flared on high, but the young men remained pure and unscathed. I should not say they 'persevered' when scripture describes them as having even walked in the midst of the furnace. Obviously they 'walked' from chastity to chastity. From each temptation they garnered immense wealth, as if they were traders coming

*Sg 2:2

*Cf. Dan 3

back from the market enriched with incomparable and irreplaceable treasure.

The whole fire is turned back on the heads of the Chaldeans, that is, the evil spirits; yet the flame did not touch in the slightest those whom, under angelic protection, the goad of concupicence did not push to consent. For to have touched is to have consented or to have been lured into consent. I myself have seen, and it has filled me with wonder, how some, newly come to monastic life, have entered the house of the Lord bearing that treasure whole and entire in their earthern vessels. After probing their conscience with considerable care, I saw clearly the glory of God, because in the furnace of fire, as I have declared quite confidently, the fire did not touch them or hurt them or give them any trouble.* This fills me not only with admiration but with delight. I shall not regard their course with the gnawing envy of the king of Babylon, of whom it is written: The wicked shall see and shall be angry.* Indeed, the intensity of his astonishment and the stab of his anguish wrung an acknowledgment from the king of Babylon, but for my part, contemplating with pure attention the appearance and the garb of these boys of ours, I have broken forth into a cry of praise from sheer joy in this holy occupation.

*Dn 3:50

*Ps 111:10

But very few, except the simple and the deeply humble, attain the glory of this kind of virtue. These lilies do not easily take root elsewhere than in secluded valleys.

*Sg 2:1

'I am a rose of Sharon,' says the spouse, 'and a lily of the valleys'.* Not only [a lily] of the valleys, but of the most sheltered valleys. Added to native simplicity is also eagerness and love for humility. They hide their treasure from human eyes, more than that, even from their own eyes. They abhor conceit as much as pride. Their eyes are lovely, like a dove's, unforgettable with the gracious beauty of their modesty and simplicity. They blush to have their treasure noticed, as though it were something stolen. The weight of this modesty is extremely heavy. It cannot bear to have another notice, let alone admire, it. This is why our young men, before they escaped the furnace of Babylon, despised the adoration of the huge golden calf the king had set up. For what is this great statue except the deceitful and enormous wickedness of pride? Blessed indeed are they who have not bent the knee before that idol and prostrated themselves before Satan in his glory. Over every danger purity triumphs, but only the purity of those who continue perseveringly in a humble steadfastness and a steadfast humility.

4. Then there is the snowy whiteness of those restored to grace through penance. Though it cannot compete on equal terms with the previous whiteness, still, it has a glory of its own, and that considerable. The virgins enjoy their privileges unimpaired; my Lord Jesus feeds among the lilies, and without let or hindrance the

lilies breathe out to him their fragrance. But our share of the radiant whiteness lies in this: we become vile in our own eyes as we contemplate their beauty, yet in proportion as we rejoice in their glory, our share in it becomes richer. Charity and humility grow, because from those partaking of this grace, we hold partnership in the same grace. This growth was more secure in their hands than in ours, for we guarded it less faithfully. Lord, it is good for me that you have humiliated me.* Manifold effects of this good have come about in me. How great is the benefit that pride, my most powerful enemy, has been swallowed up! It is not for me any more to hold my head high, not for me any more to open my mouth, because of my shame! Should I wish to justify myself, my mouth would condemn me. There is even greater benefit in the fact that, as one sought out on a dunghill by the Lord himself, removed from it, washed and made spotless, I have found abundant cause for never-failing love. In the sight of my Lord, I lack only this, that the due effect should follow the cause. I am a rich man if I lay loving hold on him who pities me, him by whom I am lovingly held.* If there is no possibility at all of a change for the better, let there at least be no change for the worse!

To sum up, then, I am not without whiteness, for the hand of the Lord has touched, cleansed, and purified me. What God has made clean, beware lest you call unclean.* You will wash me, O Lord,

*Ps 118:71

*Cf. Ph 3:12

*Ac 10:15

with your clean water, and I shall be utterly clean; you will wash me, and I shall be whiter than snow.* If my sins be made white as snow,† according to the words of Isaiah, so that the humility of penance makes up for the dignity of lost purity, then this in itself is my great comfort and my source of grace. And to enrich the source still further, God in his mercy has added a radiance even whiter than snow, so that charity may catch up to humility and snow become as wool. What was white because of the tears of penitence becomes warm as well because of the covering of charity. The new whiteness is already so superior to snow that snow itself is endued with the whiteness and warmth of wool. So when Isaiah said: 'If your sins are as scarlet, they shall be made as white as snow,'* he added immediately: 'If they are as crimson, they shall become white as wool.'* David briefly rounds out the meaning of this by saying: 'He gives snow like wool.'* Great and inestimable treasures of snow, through which garments dark and stained are made white as snow! Not only do the angels clothe themselves therein, rejoicing with great joy over one repentent sinner, but Solomon himself in all his glory deigned so to be clad.* I am speaking about that Solomon who, when he revealed the glory of his resurrection during the transfiguration on the mountain, showed his garments 'radiant like snow.'* 'Have you entered,' he says, 'the treasure houses of the snow?'* They are hidden and

*Ps 50:7*
†Is 1:18

*Is 1:18*

*Is 1:18*

*Ps 147:18*

*Cf. Mt 6:29*

*Cf. Mk 9:3*

*Jb 38:22*

exceedingly rich, and in them is very great hope of salvation. But more hidden and richer still are the treasure houses of white wool, which make whiter than snow those who have been whitened by snow, and clothe those ascending from the laver of repentence with the most radiant robe of divine love.

5. The fourth innocence, which I mentioned above, is not of this age. Whether I was right to call it the radiance of light, you can judge for yourselves. Milk can go bad and the lily wither and snow become dirty, but no defilement can come into light. It will be inseparable from the man it glorifies, clinging to him like a robe of glory,* breathing forth innocence and containing within its own circumference the brightness of its holiness. For all eternity it will not see corruption, nor in the ages yet to come experience any diminution of its radiance. That garment of light is a garment indeed, a luminous garment, subject to no darkness, not afraid of spot or wrinkle, moth or wrinkle, burn or cut or anything similar. For it will know no trouble from the spot of another's evil or the wrinkle of its own duplicity, from the inborn moth of pride or the fretting old age of discontent, from the devouring burn of concupiscence or the cut of spite or discord.

    *Si 38:22*

The first to be clothed in this white robe is that young man, fairest among the sons of men,* who first of all triumphed over death and put on splendor, so that with reason the bride glories in him uniquely

    *Ps 45:2*

and says: 'My beloved is all radiant.' He is
the first, I repeat, and up to now perhaps
the only one. For as to the resurrection of
others, whether it may have been fully
solemnized in some, the church prefers
at present a reverent hesitation rather than
a rash assertion of what cannot be proved.†
For the rest, let the case be what it will,
his whiteness is doubtlessly very unique,
for all the others receive their radiance from
his. Indeed, on the day of glory, stars will
unfold their light in the splendor of the
saints and shine to the Lord with gladness,
but if you compare a star to the sun, how
small is it? It is true that star differs from
star in brightness,* but this is before the
sun appears. Once the sun has risen, all the
stars soon go into hiding, yielding their
light to the sun as if confessing that the sun
alone gives light, and in his sight all shining
things are dim.

Well, therefore, does the bride, clinging
with longing to the face of her sun; well and
wisely does she say: 'My beloved is all
radiant'. All others derive their radiance
from him, and in comparison with him they
are hardly radiant at all. He himself is
whiter than milk, brighter than the lily,
purer than snow, more lucent than the
light. He is distinguished among thousands,*
and from him to his whole church emanates
all the radiance there is. It comes from
him and it returns to him. He is the most
innocent of little ones. He entered his
mother's womb without violating her virginity and he left it without her feeling

†John is evidently
very hesitant to
accept the doc-
trine of the
bodily assump-
tion of Our Lady.
It was not to be
defined until
our own day.
Cf. St Bernard,
Ep. 174, to the
canons of Lyons.

*1 Co 15:41

*Sg 5:10

any pain, bestowing true incorruptibility
in his conception and true joy in his birth.†
He is the flower of youth, the lily of young
men. He had no need of the seclusion of
solitude to protect his innocence, but
openly showing tenderness to the world
and the company of sinners, like the
flower of the field and the lily of the
valleys he drew all things to himself by the
power of his radiance and his fragrance. He
is the only true white one among the penitent. Of the human race he alone is found
both innocent and penitent at the same
time. He knew no sin, yet for the sake of
each and every one he was 'poured out
like water,'* and made of his own self a
laver for the purifying of sinners. He is the
glory of the resurrected, both as taking
possession of the first fruits of the resurrection and as providing through his own
personal glorification the reason for the
resurrection of all. Therefore truly radiant
and chosen among thousands is he who has
radiance of every description and of his
fullness has power to communicate to
whomever he pleases, as much as he pleases,

> Jesus Christ Our Lord,
> who with the Father
> and the Holy Spirit
> lives and reigns,
> one God,
> for ever
> and
> ever.
> Amen.

†*A patristic
tradition had it
that the virgin
birth must have
been painless.*

*\*Ps 22:14*

## SERMON FOUR

*The beginning of the fourth sermon.* Of the
four kinds of redness, that is, of blushing;
the first, namely that of pentitents, the
second of the chaste, the third of those
struggling for the truth, the fourth of those
burning with the love of Christ. And these
are described under a fourfold image of
redness: vermilion, the rose, blood, and
the ruby.

M Y BELOVED IS ALL RADIANT
and ruddy, distinguished among
thousands.'* The delightful
colors white and red become even more
delightful in combination. They set each
other off to achieve the fullness of beauty.
The radiant white makes the red stand out,
the red makes the white more intense.
Whiteness brings charm, redness joy, to the
perfection of loveliness. Indeed, without a
dash of red, whiteness verges on pallor; and
red unmixed with white inclines to the
sombre. Thus, each is a good color, but in
conjunction they are especially good, above
all in him who is the highest goodness,
uniquely beautiful. In contemplating and
admiring both colors the heart of the bride
begins to glow for her spouse, and she
receives from them together a twofold

*Sg 5:10*

111

wound of holy love. In one her beloved is splendid, in the other he is beautiful. By his splendor and beauty, as by a two-edged sword, he pierces his chosen one with great wounds which nothing will heal. 'Gird, o mighty one,' she says, 'your sword upon your thigh.'* What kind of sword, you ask? 'Your splendor and your beauty.'* Truly your sword, o mighty one, o truly your sword and a mighty sword, Lord Jesus, is your splendor and your beauty! This is a sword not of iron but of flame, showing the path to the tree of life. It acts as guardian and door-keeper to the paradise of my God, and admits none to the enjoyment of true happiness unless he be first transfixed and consumed by sacred fire. Gird, my Lord, gird on that sword of yours and use it on us, too. May we also fall by the edge of the sword, with wonder and longing for your splendor and beauty piercing to the inmost depths of our being. Light up, illuminate, show in all its brightness your face, radiant and ruddy, distinguished among thousands!

Who will grant me that my mighty Lord may draw from his sheath his irrevocable sword and stab me through with wound upon wound, until my soul dies of this precious death, a living death, the death of those pining for the living God? Alas, for the most part my spirit is still within me! It is I, still I who live,* and my flesh does not yet pine so that my heart faints for you, o God of my heart.* I go about wretched and poor. I seek on all sides,

*Ps 44:3

*Ps 45:3

*Ga 2:20

*Ps 73:26

sad and anxious, for some help in my
so that if there is any little spark of love in
my cold heart, it may be kept alive and
sheltered. Your favored virgin comes before
me, wholly dissolved in your love, pro-
claiming sweetly and abundantly the memory of the abundance of your sweetness,
speaking of ineffable joys, as far as it is
lawful for man to speak of them.* 'The        *Cf. 2 Co 12:4
only Son, who is in the bosom of his
Father,'* she does not fear to call her         *Jn 1:18
beloved, and him on whom the angels long
to gaze she experiences as her own peculiar
happiness. The bride of my Lord overflows
with noble words,* and from the overflow      *Cf. Ps 45:1
of her fullness I have perhaps derived a
little fragrance. So I can say to myself, like
a man awakening from a deep sleep* and       *Gn 45:26
breathing again a brighter hope: 'How long
will you lie there, o sluggard?* How long      *Pr 6:9
will you slowly waste away of hunger in
the midst of such great plenty? Behold
how the bride receives her beautiful beloved, how utterly he satisfies her, how
intensely she devotes herself to this one
most blessed concern, how her whole
occupation is to love Jesus.' All this can
happen secretly, all can be done in hidden-
ness in the bed chamber, as befits the joys
of lovers. But the Holy Spirit still thinks us
worthy of a share in so great a mystery that,
through the testimony of the Lord's bride,
the spirit of love should overwhelm those
who hear the word of love. And yet she
herself speaks to us in parables, unless the
Lord Jesus makes all clear and the Holy

Spirit sheds his illumination. For who is worthy to understand, who worthy to proclaim aloud, this radiance and this redness of the most beautiful of the sons of men?

2. Nevertheless, through the image of visible things, let us give some picture, however inadequate, of things thus holy and remote from sense perception. Let us, if you will, compare to the above mentioned four whitenesses the same number of red shades, that there may be a balanced mixture, a seemly blend of these distinct colors in the face of the beloved. Therefore, for instance, let there be blended together the red of vermilion, the red of the rose, the red of blood, and the red of the ruby. Perhaps they seem coarse and beneath the majesty of such great beauty, but the bride should remember—and also those maidens who are in her company and under her care that Jesus as a baby was wrapped in coarse swaddling bands by his humble mother. If he advanced in age and glory, he remains always the same in his humility, and the years of Jesus' poverty and lowliness will never come to an end. But I set these shades of red in the sunlight that, being spread out to view, they may glow more brightly. The first red is penitential shame, the second virginal modesty, the third that of the strivers for justice, the fourth of those burning with love.

3. And indeed, the redness of vermilion, of scarlet, seems to have been expressed by Isaiah, when he said: 'If my sins be as scarlet, they shall become white as

wool,'* for this is the color that suffuses
the face of the repentent sinner. How
precious is this red that covers the whole
countenance and makes it ruddy with
shame and radiant with holiness! In the
same way, we sing joyfully of the blood of
the lamb, that these are they who have
washed their robes in it and made them
white.* Quite certainly they first made
those very robes red in that same blood.
But more of this later. Consequently, the
red of this shame is good, able to temper
the former look of the discolored face and
to restore my inborn radiance.

4. O my God, the salvation of my
countenance,* when shall I confess to you
in the simplicity of my heart what I owe
you as your just tribute? For you have
begun to wipe away from my face the dis-
figuring stains with which I have marred it,
you have begun to breathe into it, with a
fresh outpouring of grace, the breath of
life which I had blown out. In short, you
have hung in my face a ruddy cloud to protect me from the heat of fiery passion, and
now and then with a shower of healing
rain to wash away what sin has befouled.
Alas, why have I had the insane desire to
hide from the face of my God, because I
was naked?* Why did I not rather hear,
though from a far distant land, a voice
from heaven advising me: 'Look to him
and be radiant, and your face will never be
ashamed?* Woe is me that my sojourning
in that land was prolonged!* Although it is
late, by his mercy and at his summons,

*Is 1:18

*Rv 7:14

*Ps 42:5

*Cf. Gn 3:10

*Ps 34:5
*Ps 120:6

I have yet drawn near. Because he has shed the light of his face upon me, the shadows have begun to melt from my face and a new light to arise and to grow slowly ever brighter. Good, therefore, is the red of this vermilion, which draws away the shadows from the face of the abyss, by its light making even the thickest shadows become like the noon-day.

Then, what of the fact that we see the very appearance of our books brightened by this color, and the important letters used as chapter headings usually outlined in it? Clearly, the page of our whole behavior will be silent and unsightly, especially to the eyes of the inward reader, unless animated by the vivid color of this shame. 'The just man,' says Solomon, 'is first of all an accuser of himself.'* Ambrose, we well know, says the same: 'May this day be spent happily, may shame be like the daybreak.'† And probably it is enough for the just man to be first of all the accuser of himself, but for me it is not enough.'I have nothing to cover my nakedness from the eyes of God if I cast aside the sackcloth of penance with which he covered me when the robbers left me stripped and bare. In this present life I will hold fast to my breast the sackcloth thrown down to me from heaven, I will make it my breast-band. Under its cover and protection, o Lord, I can hide from the face of your wrath. It will be of your mercy that you will make me fit for a softer and more festal robe, and that will be when you call me to the

*Pr 18:17

†A quotation from the hymn Splendor paternae gloriae by St Ambrose sung at Lauds by Cistercians.

marriage feast and wish to distinguish me with a special breast-band. Yet that is the only way I would be happy to divest myself of the first wrapping, very mindful of how, in the Lord's tabernacle, rough sackcloth is draped over the material, to keep the glory of the hangings safe from storm and rain. But this has not yet happened. Although my Lord has put on splendor, he has not taken off the confession in which he first deigned to clothe himself.* And this is what is to be said of the first redness.

*\*Cf. Ps 93:1*

5. Now, if the power of shame or this redness be so great, what a boon, think you, will be that which reddens the cheek of virgins? As we read: 'A modest woman is a boon twice over.'* If she is blessed whose sins are covered over,* how much more blessed is she whose very merits are so carefully covered over? The former ruddiness concerned guilt, but this concerns grace and protects glory with a canopy. 'Over all the glory', says Isaiah, 'there will be a canopy.'* So this modesty, too, is a cloud, covering and protecting, a cloud overshadowing the virginal face in case the sun by day should scorch it, the face that is, of one who glories not in himself but in the Lord.

*\*Sir 26:19*
*\*Ps 32:1*

*\*Is 4:5*

So it was with Mary, most blessed of women and chief of virgins. After she had been promised the fulness of grace, after she had been told that Christ would be born of her and the Holy Spirit poured out, then finally, last of all, the promise was

made of the overshadowing. According to
Isaiah, this was in order to have a great
canopy over so great a glory. 'The power',
it says, 'of the Most High shall overshadow
*Lk 1:35*  you.'* And what is the power of the Most
High overshadowing the mother if not that
which brought the Most High down to a
mother's womb and breasts? Obviously,
humility is the power of the virgin, high
above all others, because its greatness becomes the height and makes them high in
very deed. But in a special way it should be
called the power of the Most High, because
in the beginning it drew him down from the
heights to the depths, and after he had
emptied himself, drew him up once more
to the right hand of his Father. So, according to the word of the angel, it was this
virtue that overshadowed the blessed virgin, as one set on the loftiest pinnacle of
power. Humility covered her continually
with the veil of holy modesty, so that she
could not be touched by the slightest sen-
sation of pride. And not only she, but
those virgins whom she attracts by the
scent of her holy virginity and leads to the
king, they too cultivate in their gardens the
same slips of the rose.

Finally, from the depth of bashfulness
must also be reckoned the depth of
chastity, and usually, the readier a face is
to blush, the greater its strength in purity.
There is an inseparable and wholly indissoluble bond between the two; indeed, the
one word 'modesty' is common to them
both. It is the special mark of bashfulness

that, like a mother and nurse, it shares the advantages of its name with chastity, or rather, makes them common property. So, o consecrated virgins, take great care to vie with the mother of the Lord and our queen in this gift of grace. As you blush at the address of man, so, too, you should mistrust the greeting of an angel promising the fulness of grace. Generally speaking, the more flatteringly a greeting toasts our health, the more insidiously it undermines our health, as Solomon testified, saying that this kind of blessing resembled a curse.* *\*Pr 27:14* To keep your lilies perpetually white, let them be walled around by the never-fading redness of this kind of rose. If at any time your faces blush, let them redden with good reason. Faithfully keep guard over your eyes, ears, lips—in short, all your bodily senses—so that death may never creep in and put his hand to the hidden treasure.

6. At this point the mind call dwell perplexed on that bashfulness which we have attributed to those striving for the truth, since Truth himself says: 'Whoever is ashamed of me and my words, of him will I be ashamed in the presence of my Father.'* In like manner Paul, inciting *\*Lk 9:26* Timothy to the combat and throwing off the burden of this redness, says: 'Do not be ashamed of testifying to Jesus Christ,'* *\*2 Tm 1:18* He frankly acknowledges in his own regard: 'I am not ashamed of the gospel.'* But it is *\*Rm 1:16* obviously one thing to be ashamed of Christ, and quite another to be ashamed for

Christ or on his account. There is no doubt
that this is the cry of the martyrs: 'All the
day long my shame is before me.'* They
were intensely ashamed when Christ was
blasphemed in their hearing and once more
reputed with the wicked, and when in the
mouth of blasphemers, God-and-man became a worm and no man, scorned by
men and despised by the people.* So it is
shame or bashfulness which, crushed by
insults, succumbs to the torture or even
before it, and it is shame or bashfulness
which, provoked by obloquy, is all the
more roused up and armed for the battle.
Perhaps, even as they enter the arena,
human nature being what it is, they may
be seized with dread, begin greatly to fear
and to say: 'My heart is like melting wax,'*
and then they receive heavenly strength
and say: 'My courage is dry like a shield.'*
It is just the same today. When the imi-
tators of the martyrs are dishonored by
some wicked insult for the sake of justice,
or for no reason at all, it is not without
severe shame that they receive the wounds
to their good name, though everything
within them may be unharmed. O good
Jesus, how wearisome is that night, how
full of anguish and conflict, since not even
the lightsome testimony of conscience,
shining in secret, is able to illuminate that
darkness!

7. Whoever suffers martyrdom, therefore, let him be steadfast. Without any
doubt there is a reward for his labor, and
that a very rich one. This is a distress that

*Ps 44:15

*Ps 22:6

*Ps 22:14

*Ps 22:15

leads to glory; for the time being endure
with patience that it covers your face for a
little. Take confidently, as from a Father's
hand, the cup which your Father has given
you as his fatherly gift. Drink it confidently. If the taste is bitter, the effect is
wholly life-giving. Yet take care not to
describe as wickedly forced on you by
your brother what is in fact graciously
tendered by your Father! Be careful to
temper it discreetly for yourself with water
drawn in joy from the fountains of salvation,* so that the cup may come to you       *Ps 74:15
from the Lord's hand, full of pure wine. At
the invocation of the Lord Jesus, the
blessing of heaven will have changed the
cup of wrath to a cup of grace. It will have
become an intoxicating cup, bringing complete forgetfulness of all that wearies,* a    *Ps 23:5
cup most precious, ushering in the happiness of everlasting hope.

8. Last of all, what, without inade-
quacy, can be said of the bashful shame
felt by those who love Christ? What can
make them blush whose life is Christ,
whose experience is Christ, in short, to
whom everything is Christ? Have we not
the word of her spouse that the bride of
Christ is wholly beautiful? Has the charity
of Christ not wiped away all stain from
her face, not smoothed away all wrinkle?
But plainly the bride of Christ finds occasion in the behavior of other people,
though not in her own, to blush and
lament. Who sins, and she does not grieve?
Who has cause to be ashamed, and she is

not overcome with confusion? Unimpeded
by burdens of her own, she graciously lends
a shoulder to bear the burdens of others.
Any kind of burden, any weight, she takes
up with joyful ease and loving kindness.
She knows from whom she has learned to
bear our sorrows and carry our griefs.*
This is truly how it is with her, as long as
the charity of Christ urges* her to the
charity of her neighbor.

9. Even in the love she bears for Christ
himself, however, the bride finds reason to
blush for shame. Quite certainly she feels
abashed at her great want of resemblance
to him, and says: 'O Lord, who is like
you?'* She feels abashed and weary because
of her imperfection. Without any hesitation she sees this as [the reason] why her
beloved did not show himself to her from
yesterday and the day before, why he is so
often called and does not reply, why he is
so diligently sought and yet keeps his face
averted from her. It does not enter her
mind to attribute to him the reasons for
her being ignored and left weary, for she
knows from experience that his goodness
is utterly good. Rather, she imposes a
penalty on herself for her lukewarmness,
she herself pays for it in full. What of the
charity of those just men of the past, who
waited and sighed for the coming of Christ?
She brings this charity, as it were, in evidence against herself, and blushes that it
has withdrawn from her, although she so
utterly rejoices in it. If the church of those
who were waiting for Jesus yearned so

*Is 53:4

*2 Co 5:14

*Ps 35:10

ardently for his kiss, impatient of delay, how can she but feel a burning shame at her own lukewarmness? She has tasted and seen, she has known his scent, she has felt his touch, she has more than once had the happiness of receiving the kiss of that most holy mouth. Yet, up to now, seeking him with great effort, she has not been worthy to make him her own.* If the fire in Sion is so great, what will the furnace in Jerusalem be?* If the bride compares her love to that of the heavenly spirits, who see the face of Jesus and long to see it with a desire that never tires and is never satisfied, then surely her little spark is not excessive?

*Cf. Ph 3:12*

*Is 31:9*

Finally, if she sets clearly before her mind her spouse's love, with which he forestalled her, how can she think her own love worth even being called love?

So the bride of Christ has in her face a special radiance and a great rosyness, one as much as the other, so that, as we said above, she may have a variety of shades enhancing her ruddiness. What do you think of the way this red gives brightness to the white, how it wounds the heart of the spouse, how it glows in the bride's cheeks, how it shines on her forehead? The precious stone hanging from the forehead is the ruby gem. This ruby throws fiery sparks from the face of the loved one to the heart of her lover. Surely it is one of the 'stones of fire'* in 'the paradise of God',* ever burning, sent to complete the bride's beauty by the Father of her spouse, our Lord Jesus Christ,

*Ezk 28:14*
*Rv 2:7*

with whom there is honor and glory
for ever
and ever.
Amen.

## SERMON FIVE

**The beginning of the fifth sermon.** That the bride calls the spouse distinguished among thousands can be taken in two ways, referring either to the whole body of holy church, or to a single member of the body. Yet in either way, the praise whether of all or of one, is to be referred to the head which is Christ.

THE TWO PREVIOUS SERMONS have considered, one of the four-fold kinds of radiance, the other the same number of different reds. But if you remember, both sermons seemed more concerned with the beauty of the bride than with the spouse, except that in the face of the bride, as in his mirror, the beauty of the spouse shines more radiantly forth. What are we to make of the fact that the beauty of each is indistinguishable and undivided? Those who are one flesh and one spirit, how are they not one beauty? O sons of men, what fools you are to exchange your glory for an idol, 'an image of an ox that eats grass!'* What good is it to you even to look at this glory soon to perish and soon after to involve you in ruin? In your eagerness for glory, why not rather turn your thoughts to the glory of the bride, [the

*Ps 106:20

125

*Cf. Ps 43:2
*Ps 48:8-9
*Jn 1:14

glory] which she has in common with her spouse? To turn your mind to it is already to become a sharer in it. For, as those who have seen have told us,* and we who have heard to truly believe,* the spouse has a glory as of the only Son of the Father,* and this he graciously pours into his bride. O truly, as the apostle witnesses, a great and solemn engagement, because of the great love, the great bond, the great union!

I think the bride has understood this, and conveyed it to the daughters of Jerusalem by adding to her praise of the radiance of her beloved and his ruddiness, that he is 'distinguished among thousands'.* For she did not say: 'My beloved is all radiant and ruddy, distinguished before thousands,' or 'distinguished in the midst of thousands,' but 'distinguished' (as she puts it) 'among thousands'. Surely she is signifying that he is distinguished by those whom he has distinguished, that he is displaying his radiant whiteness and redness to those thousands who are his own. He is indeed the 'fairest of the sons of men,'* but in the form of his beauty he is one among the sons of men. He himself makes the claim: 'All the beauty of the field is mine.'* And again: 'I am the flower of the field and the lily of the valley.'* How long, o my soul, will you be disturbed within your self all day, shut up in the narrowness of your personal poverty? Is not the Lord your God—for I do not yet dare to say your beloved or your spouse— is he not himself your beauty, your flower,

*Sg 5:10

*Ps 45:2

*Ps 50:11
*Sg 2:1

your lily? For he is not glorious only in that beauty by which he is equal to the Father, but also in that apparel which he washed in the wine of his blood. It is written: 'He is glorious in his apparel.'* *Is 63:1* I am speaking of the church of Christ. Even if before his passion it was soiled with stains and creased with wrinkles, the robe of glory prepared for it was reddened by the blood of her spouse, radiant and ruddy, and made a robe no less radiant and red, having 'no stain or wrinkle or any such thing.'* He changed it like a *Eph 5:27* garment, and it was changed,* in turn *Cf. Ps 102:27* changelessly and inseparably befitting such great splendor and majesty.

2. Consequently, there is a twofold sense in which one says: 'among thousands.' Either can be understood aright, whether it refers to a totality or to separate individuals, that is to say, whether you take it as the beauty of the whole, or of one by itself among the thousands. God is wonderful in his saints in both these ways, wonderful in all, wonderful in each.

To say something briefly about the first wonder, what is more wonderful than the binding together in his body of all creation, differentiating the parts of this body by the great law, so that, marvelously, what seems less honorable in it he surrounds, as the apostle remarks, with more glory?* *Cf. 1 Co 12:24* Does the beauty of the whole person, head as well as body, not belong to every part, even the least? Not otherwise is the glory with which he has united this same church

of his to himself in the bond of marriage.
He has redeemed her and washed her clean
in his blood, he has dowered her with the
Holy Spirit, he has, finally, even enriched
her with his own kingdom. What glory is
like this? With reason, with very good
reason, shall 'all my bones say: "Lord, who
is like you?" '* Let me repeat it: 'who is
like you?' To make one who was deformed
and dissimilar not only beautiful, but
conformed and similar to yourself, you
made yourself similar to him. You became
as one who 'had no form or comeliness.'*
Among all the marvels of God, what marvel
is equal to this, that the king of glory came
as a servant to rescue his bride from the
yoke of servitude? That from heaven he
desired her beauty, though up to now she
was black with Ethiopian ugliness? That
having sold himself into slavery to serve
more fittingly, he stripped off his beauty,
stripped off his strength, girt himself with
servile lowliness, and in every way made
himself ready and apt to wash away her
defects?

3. Have you opened wide your mouth
about him, daughter of Saul? Have you
thrust out your tongue at him, daughter of
Canaan and not of Judah? Have you
reproached the king of glory for dancing
naked before the ark? For you said, wagging
your head at him: 'How the king of Israel
honored himself today, uncovering himself
before the eyes of his servant's maids, as
one of the vulgar fellows shamelessly un-
covers himself!'* Yes, inglorious in your

*Ps 35:10

*Is 53:2

*2 Sa 6:20

eyes, blinded by the lowliness of that nakedness. But blessed are the eyes of the bride who in the total emptying of her Solomon, crowned with a crown of thorns, not only took no scandal, but all the more eagerly, all the more lovingly, ran to his embrace and threw herself into his arms! How fortunate you are, bride of God, how glorious, to be the reward of such a loving servitude, the fruit of such a long and lasting pilgrimage, the prize of such a difficult undertaking, in short, the price of his precious blood! And let no one dare to suppose that the wisdom of God was overreached in this matter. In fact, returning home to heaven from the market-place of this world of ours, he did not say that his bargain was a poor one. On the contrary, calling together his friends and neighbors, he gloried before them, and made it clear that they should congratulate him.

What could possibly increase this glory? It is no less wonderful, perhaps even more wonderful, that after the Lord reigned, robed in majesty, girded with strength,* *\*Ps 93:1* clad in the glory of his resurrection as in a garment, even then, in all this glory of his, the king of glory girded himself to serve. I lie, if from the mouth of the Truth, this promise to the disciples does not ring out in the gospel, that 'he will gird himself and have them sit at the table, and he will come and minister to them'.* If you will allow *\*Lk 12:37* me to speak to you, o Lord my God, though I am but dust and ashes, what comparable statement has ever been made by

any king, by any master to his servants? If
you will allow me, I charge you with your
own words, o Lord: 'Which is the greater,
one who sits at table or one who serves? Is
it not the one who sits at table?'* Certainly it was a mark of your inestimable
goodness to have come down to us from
heaven not to be served but to serve. But
does it still seem fitting to you, now that
you are in the day of your eternity and on
your majestic throne to come down just the
same to serve and not be served? What
more can the bride of my Lord say to you,
her Lord? She can only pay you homage
with all that is in her, and admit: 'Lord,
who is like you?'* If there is anything that
can be added to such a weight of glory, it is
this: perhaps the bride may feel a little
worried about the small number who are to
be saved. With anxiety she so often hears
her spouse repeating: 'Many are called, but
few are chosen.'* That this fear, too, may
be completely removed from her, she hears
also, with joy and exultation: 'Who can
count the number of his armies?'*

4. This too she hears: 'The chariots of
God are many thousand times ten thousand
of the rejoicing.'* If at his first ascension,
the chariot of the spouse is so many
thousands of the rejoicing, so that the huge
crowd of those triumphing with Christ
flows over into many times ten thousand,
what, I ask, will be the chariot of his second
ascension? If such is the harvest of the first-
fruits, what will be the riches of the full
harvest, when the reaper fills his hand?*

*Lk 22:27

*Ps 35:10

*Mt 20:16

*Jb 25:3

*Ps 68:17

*Ps 129:7

And fills not only his hand, but his barns
too, right up to the very top? On that day,
how will Abraham allege that anything is
missing from the promise God made to him
and to his seed, anything missing from their
shining to everlasting ages like the stars of
sky, from their wholly exceeding all reckoning in number like the sands on the
sea shore?

5. Last of all, at this point, the bride
herself does not pass over in silence the
ineffable fullness of her glory. When she
adds to her description of her beloved:
'distinguished among thousands,' she wants
to have understood by those thousands the
whole assembly of the saints. She accepts
them from the generosity of her spouse as
the gift of his great promise. 'As I live,' says
the Lord, (without doubt the words refer
to the saints and apply to the bride), 'you
will be clad with them as with adornment,
and you will take them to yourself as a
bride.'*  Who would now be astonished if      *Is 49:18
she herself is astonished, or rather, if she
sees and is rich and her astonished heart
swells with emotion? For she is enriched
with both blessings, a weight of unimaginable glory, and a countless number of
souls in glory. She has indeed found the
Lord at her desire, as the saying has it, she
has found God at her pleasure, she has
found a spouse after her own heart. And
yet he himself may say what we find in the
prophet: 'In this also, the house of Israel
will find me.'*                                *Ezk 36:37
6. But let us keep these things for a

new start, so that tomorrow they may be placed fresh before the hungry. May it never happen that you take your seat at the Lord's table other than hungry, or else wisdom, usually the consolation of weariness, as scripture says,* will herself become the cause of weariness, like drunkenness from wine. 'Who eats me,' says Wisdom, 'will still hunger,'* and the mother of Wisdom says of Wisdom: 'He fills the hungry with good things.'* So when you gather together tomorrow, hungering for the bread of the Lord's supper, the fragments of what we have broken today will provide a feast. May it be blessed by him who opens his hand and fills every living creature with blessing,* the spouse of the church, our Lord Jesus Christ, who with the Father and the Holy Spirit lives and reigns, God, for ever and ever. Amen.

*Cf. Ws 8:9

*Jn 4:13

*Lk 1:53

*Ps 145:16

## SERMON SIX

*The beginning of the sixth sermon.* Of the threefold multiplication of the saints which the Lord promises his church in the words of the prophet Ezechiel: 'I will increase them like a flock of men,'* and so on. *Ezk 36:37*

R EMEMBERING YESTERDAY'S PROMISE, here I come hastening to meet my obligation to you, my creditors. Perhaps it will not be in the measure you demand and I ought to pay, but it is the measure for the present measured out to me by God. So in this respect I ask you to be patient with me, and when God has expanded me, then I too, will be expansive towards you!

That saying of the prophet in yesterday's sermon went no further in discussing the multiplication of the saints than: 'In this, also, the house of Israel will find me,' The whole quotation goes: 'I will increase them like a flock of men, like the flock for sacrifices, like the flock of Jerusalem during her appointed feasts. In this, also, the house of Israel will find me.'* The bride *Ezk 36:37* first found him, blessedly and unexpectedly, when she was anticipated by him with blessings of sweetness and raised to the bond of marriage, even to the delights of

133

the nuptial chamber and a partnership in his kingdom. In the end, however, she heaps together all other blessings in this most rich and joyful blessing, which he who blesses enumerates as increasing in a threefold way.

2. 'It will increase them', he says, 'like a flock of men, like the flock for sacrifice, like the flock at Jerusalem during her appointed feasts.' Now, unless you have a better idea, I think the 'flock of men' is that multitude of the faithful who have turned away from the likeness of animals, and have either preserved by grace or repaired by penance the image of God within them to which man was created. In fully human fashion, that is, living sober, upright and godly lives in this world,* they look forward confidently to the blessed hope promised to the faithful. And I put it to you: what is it like, what is its size, this great crowd of so many generations of peoples, tribes and tongues? From so many ages past even unto now, it has been gathered together, and it must still be gathered up to the very end of time. What delight will be yours, o bride of God, when all these have come to you in assembly, when that flock of so many thousand men, new and marked [with a sign], display before your eyes the image of God, clearly marked on their countenance, and in every face, as in the brightest of mirrors, you see and adore your creator?

3. Lift your eyes higher still, to another fruit of a fresh harvest, to the 'flock for the

*Tt 2:12

sacrifice' which the Lord your God is going
to bestow on you. In my opinion, these are
they who, in order to become holy and
once holy to become holier still, have
entered upon the path of a consecrated
life. Each has taken hold of his neighbor's
right hand and said to one another: 'Come,
let us go up to the mountain of the
Lord!'* According to the angel's counsel, *Is 2:3*
we shall more easily be saved on the
mountain—or rather, according to the
counsel of the great angel of great counsel,
that is, the Lord Jesus, the only road to
perfection for us is to leave all things and
follow Jesus.* Therefore, at the sound of *Lk 5:11*
this word, which the rich man would
scarcely listen to when Jesus spoke it*— *Cf. Mt 19:22*
and it is even written of him there that
after he had listened to it, he went away
sorrowful—an infinite multitude have
opened their ears, have risen up with joy,
have run eagerly forward. Abruptly snap-
ping all the ties that could hold them back,
they have suffered the loss of everything
that is of this world, even the loss of their
own will, so as to fill up the ranks of the
kingdom of heaven. The advance guard of
this multitude were those in the very
beginning of the primitive church of whom
it is written: They were of one heart and
soul.* Truly, this is the flock for the Lord's *Ac 4:32*
sacrifice. For the sake of Christ they resign
all worldly advantage through voluntary
poverty, they despise all delight in sensual
pleasure through the perpetual strength of
chastity, they deny every inclination of

their own will through the free love of
obedience. Who would think this holy flock
can even be numbered since, leaving aside
the men of ages past, we can see them this
very day increasing like the stars of heaven?
And this increases your happiness, o bride
of the Lord Jesus; all this is your adornment, the banner of your loveliness, the
bounty of your bridal dower!

4. Rise up yet higher, stand on the
heights and lift up your eyes. Turning, you
will see a flock with a glory more excellent
still, the flock clearly pre-eminent, 'the
flock at Jerusalem during her appointed
feasts'. These are the great friends of God,
exceedingly honored, overwhelmingly con-
soled. Here the patriarchs hold the first
rank,* because God bequeathed to them
his covenant and magnified his mercy. So
from them all holy fatherhood on earth
takes its name, making them not only the
fathers of all who believe, but also the an-
cestors of Christ according to the flesh.
Following them come the venerable company of the prophets, aware of the hidden
things of God and explaining them to the
sons of men. Even in those days they
preached to the world what we now, with
our own eyes, see fulfilled in us, and to
which we look forward to contemplating,
after a little, in all its wholeness. Next to
them is the glorious company of the
apostles, by whose preaching the world
was saved, through whose government the
world is ruled, at whose tribunal the world
will be judged. Then the impenetrable and

*Cf. the hymn
Te Deum *for
ranks of
witnesses.*

uncountable army of martyrs, marked with
so many of the wounds of Christ, refined
to purity by the fire of many tortures,
carrying into heaven many banners of
victory. After them the pastors and doc-
tors, who by their teaching and example, by
their signs and wonders, made the catholic
faith and the christian religion shine forth
more brightly than the light, indeed, like
the splendor of the starry sky. Finally the
virgins, whiter than snow, following their
spouse wherever he goes, and most of
these, not content with a single glory, have
also washed red with martyrs' blood their
robes of radiant virginity. Who begot in
you these men of such great glory, o fruitful mother, o bride of the king of glory?
Truly that flock of yours is a joyful flock,
a festive flock, establishing for you a festal
procession with branches,* and that for
ever. They have even added more feasts, as
many as the indescribable reasons they have
for eternal happiness. However ample your
lap, however wide you open your mouth,
still the Lord has power to fill it to overflowing with the good things of his house.
They are so great and manifold that you
will say: 'O Lord, you have visited the
earth and watered it, you have made it
very rich;'* 'Your grace is sufficient for
me;'† 'I have no more vessels'* in which
anything can be poured; your torrent has
filled my heart with waters,* in fact, they
brim over and overflow my lap.

    5. Although up to now we have been
discussing the bride's glory, if you remem-

*Ps 118:27*

*Ps 65:9*
†2 Co 12:9
*2 K 4:6*

*Cf. Ps 65:9*

*Ps 111:4

ber, she herself, on a fit occasion made a memorial of his wonderful works.* She spoke of her beloved to the daughters of Jerusalem, saying of him that he was 'all radiant and ruddy', and adding, 'distinguished among thousands'. We took this as referring to the universal beauty of the church, as if the bride were to say: 'Indeed my beloved is wonderful in his saints and beautiful in each individually, but he is far more wonderful in his whole body, that is, distinguished among the thousands that are his own.'

6. On the other hand, if it seems better to take her words 'distinguished among thousands' as meaning distinguished among each one separately, then it can also bear this meaning. We refer to the whole body in its totality when we sing in the psalms: 'With the holy you show yourself holy, with the blameless you show yourself blameless, with the distinguished you show yourself distinguished.'* But perhaps it is not the same thing to be distinguished 'with' the distinguished as to be distinguished 'among' the distinguished. In one, God is present by cooperating grace; in the other, God is within by indwelling power. One we yearn after, to receive; the other we breathe in, not to lose. Finally, in another place it is written: 'You dwell in the sanctuary, the praise of Israel.'* What flock, however little it may be, is not blessed, and blessed, too, each little member of the flock, who has such a great one as this to distinguish it? God himself is

*Ps 18: 25-26

*Ps 22:3

distinguished in him. Blessed is the man whom you distinguish, O Lord,* yet the one chosen for distinction is more blessed still when you give him your aid in doing good. And he is most blessed of all when you repose in him as in your own home, and say: 'Here is my resting place for ever, here I dwell for I have distinguished it.'* Now, O Lord, Father and Ruler of my life,* give me the wisdom that sits by your throne,* the Lord Jesus, that he may be with me and toil, and that I may learn what is pleasing to you,* standing before you at all times.* May he be with me, stirring up my dullness. May he labor with me, helping on my weakness, and so that I do not stub my toe as I walk through my darkness, may he shed his light upon my ignorance.

7. Yet, even though you walk with me like this and take hold of my right hand, your indwelling grace is indispensable: that is to say, your mercy, that it may follow me all the days of my life.* I have in fact enemies, all the more evil in that they are interior. They dwell within me, they lurk there, they lie in wait in my inmost depths, especially the spirit of vanity, the spirit of ingratitude, and the spirit of swelling passion. Hence it is in every way absolutely indispensable for me that the strength of Christ should dwell within me to free me from what surges up from my own heart. Otherwise, I should foolishly glory in your good things as though they were mine, taking the glory to myself, or else ungratefully giving you

*Ps 65:4

*Ps 132:14
*Si 23:1

*Ws 9:4

*Ws 9:10
*2 Ch 9:4

*Ps 23:6

no glory for your good things, as though they were not graces received from you, or else, though thanking you, I should not know enough to give you glory in company with my brothers, but would want to contract you, common source of all goodness, to my own private happiness. These intimate enemies of mine are a very great danger to my salvation, and they are your enemies, too, Lord God, throwing off your right hand and taking away from your glory. O Protector of mankind, from them, I beg you, protect me as the apple of your eye, for the sake of our salvation, which is you yourself! Otherwise, all I achieve of myself, will be—which God forbid—like chaff which the wind drives away!*

*Ps 1:4*

Opposed to this inward and furtive ugliness is the inner and most clean beauty of the truth in all its fair purity. It is of this that the psalmist speaks to the Lord: I know, o Lord, that your judgements are right, and in your truth you have laid my pride low.* And again: I have taken pleasure in your truth.* For it is this that takes away all stain of vanity, and humbly acknowledges the grace of God. It is this that drives out every mark of thanklessness, and earnestly gives grace its full glory. It is this that heals all the swelling of individualism and shares grace in the company of the brethren and wants it to be common to all. This is obviously the treasure, worthy of our longing, which the 'distinguished among thousands' lays up as

*Ps 119:75*
*Ps 26:3*

a treasure for himself. This is the desirable beauty which he, the beautiful one, desires in the king's daughter. This, if I am not mistaken, is the ineffable secret of the bride's beauty, which the spouse has not wished to leave entirely undescribed, and yet has not wished to describe in any fulness. 'Your eyes are doves', he says to the bride, 'behind your veil.'* As much as possible, the 'distinguished among thousands' has kept this behind the veil and buried it deep in the hiding-place of his heart. He has laid it up as a treasure for himself alone and has concealed it from the harm of any eye, in case the proud should speak lies against it.

*Sg 4:1

8. But delve still more deeply into the words of the bride. Commending his grace and dignity among his chosen ones, she does not say, chosen 'by' him, nor chosen 'in' him, though both are true and a sign of his inestimable grace. But what she says is, chosen (or distinguished) 'among' them, and so makes his grace stand out as more gracious and loving. They were indeed chosen 'by' him before time began, when together with the Father he, of his free goodness, arranged beforehand the matter of their salvation. They were chosen 'in' him when he freely settled with the Father the means and form of their salvation. But because she says that he himself was chosen 'among' them, she shows forth rather the dignity of receiving than the largess of bestowing.

Take it that the bride, applying herself

with even greater zeal to the praises of her
beloved, has addressed the daughters of
Jerusalem as follows: Why do you question
me about my beloved, what he is like?
Consider the lilies of the field, look at the
roses, lift up your eyes on all sides and
open them wide and see thousands of his
choice distinguished ones blossoming with
the flowers of different virtues! Yet my
beloved alone is radiant in them, he alone
is ruddy in them, in short, he alone is
chosen, is distinguished in them! Why
look with envy, o many-peaked mountains?* Let arrogance not come forth from
your mouth,* because there is no other
my beloved, and there is none holy and
none distinguished save only he. 'Behold
my Son'—without any doubt the Father is
speaking of the beloved. 'Behold,' he says,
'my chosen one whom I have chosen,* in
whom my soul delights.'*

9. And now, Lord, remember me when
you show favor to your people,* and may
he in whom your soul delights not find my
soul no delight to him! Look upon the face
of your Christ,* living and moving in us
through your grace, and since it is through
him that you save us, save your king,* save
your Christ, who lives and makes his abode
in us! To make certain that you will listen,
he himself intercedes with you from within
us on our behalf; he himself groans to you,
his Father; he himself, from the ends of the
earth, from all the deep places of our hearts,
cries out to you in supplication, Abba,
Father! I ask you, how can you deny at

*Ps 68:16
*1 Sa 2:3

*Mt 12:18
*Is 42:1

*Ps 106:4

*Cf. Ps 84:9

*Ps 20:9

least a hearing to him? For the sake of your servant David, for his sake who is after your own heart, do not turn away the face of your Christ!* *Ps 132:10*

Meanwhile, whoever you are who desire to be included under the name of daughters of Jerusalem, do not come to make little account of the thousands of chosen ones, because he alone among them is distinguished. On the contrary, all the more eagerly walk around Sion, go all around her,* since in Sion is the habitation of the *Ps 48:12* holy of holies. Take great and watchful care not to despise one of these thousands, not to condemn, not to scandalize anyone at all of these little ones. The many you think lowly is of a mighty stock, he has a mighty Father, a most renowned Brother, mighty friends, mighty servants. Do not look too curiously, over-rash judge, at what is unattractive on the outside! Act rather like a careful investigator, look through the windows as becomes a good friend, peep through the lattices, and take a long look at how bright it is inside. Granted there are coarse cloaks and earth-colored pelts, but have you eyes for nothing else? You should rather be looking at the ark of the Lord, hiding beneath these coverings of fleshly weakness, and then you would not be disturbed. You would begin to feel reverence, you would look, and wonder!

Listen to me even more closely still! Take very great care that it is not Jesus you are despising, clad in his dirty rags! You recall, I think, with me, that it was in such a manner that the prophet saw the Lord Jesus. Blessed is he who considers the needy and the poor,* blessed who has not been scandalized in him, whether wrapped in swaddling bands or clothed in shabby garments. Do you want to know what these things are? Let him give you the answer: 'I was hungry, I was thirsty, I was naked, I was a stranger, I was sick and in prison.'* These pelts have indeed the color of red earth, because they are reddened with the blood of suffering. Infirmities, especially of the body, are, however mean, as it were the garments of the Lord Jesus.

10. But more difficult and burdensome by far are the hidden privations of the mind in its interior struggles. These are like the cloaks of sacking thrown around beggers, garments much more poverty-stricken than the former. Nevertheless, with these, too, the king of glory was quite willing to be covered. So bend an attentive ear to wisdom, your mother, as she faithfully advises you: 'When you gain a friend, gain him through testing.'* And who, I put it to you, is a more faithful friend than Jesus, more helpful or more gracious? And who, I put it to you, is at this time more dishonored, weak or suffering? We know that king Solomon in his splendor and glory was highly esteemed, and yet, behold here a greater than Solomon,* one with the power to build for himself a temple of gold and precious stones, should he so wish, when and how he wishes. But meanwhile, dwelling in these pelts and clad in this kind

*Ps 41:1

*Cf. Mt 25:35-36

*Si 6:7

*Mt 12:42

of garment, what he wishes is to ask us a
question, whether we truly know and love
him so disguised and even, if one dare say
it, so dirty. Blessed beyond doubt are those
who will hear him say on that day: 'You
are those who have continued with me in
my trials. In the past you recognized and
knew me wrapped in tatters, you were not
ashamed of my chains, you refreshed me
in my battles with weakness and poverty.
Behold, as my Father has appointed me a
kingdom, so do I appoint one for you.*     *Cf. Lk 22:29*
From this time forth and for ever more,*     *Is 9:7*
your eyes will see the king in his beauty.'*     *Is 33:17*

He will reign with God the Father
and the Holy Spirit,
for ever and ever.
Amen.

## SERMON SEVEN

*The beginning of the seventh sermon.* Of the irreverence of those who presume to argue about the eternal generation of Christ; how the daughters of Jerusalem ask about it not curiously but humbly, seeking not so much after profundity as consolation. How the bride satisfies their questions under a figure yet quite adequately, the figure of radiance and redness, that is, of light and heat. Of the different properties of light and heat.

DEAREST BRETHREN, I have heard your complaint, on behalf of the daughters of Jerusalem, that their desires were not satisfied nor a proper answer given to their questions. In fact, had I not learned the explanation of this from the lips of the bride herself, it would have been a hard task for me to undo what was tied with so tricky a knot. I would have had to struggle to understand the nature of the desire and the minds of those who desired it. To begin with, then, I see the question itself as repeated not without good reason. The repetition is obviously in order to elicit a conversation, as well as to express anxious and ardent devotion. The first part of the question runs like this: 'What is your beloved more

147

*Sg 1:9
†Sg 1:9

than another beloved, o fairest among women?'* The second part says: 'What is your beloved, that you thus adjure us?'† This leaves out the words added to the end of the first part, namely: 'more than another beloved.' Of course, there is a deep reason behind the mysteries that are really spoken by the spirit, the spirit of charity. At least, this is so for those who can comprehend, that is, those who have the grace to savor him, for certainly they alone understand this language.

Anyhow, to my way of thinking, in their first question—'What is your beloved more than another beloved?'—the daughters of Jerusalem did not want the bride to deign to disclose to them anything about the glory of the spouse. Their question did not refer to that supreme glory which he possesses as the only Son of the Father. They take it for granted that she would consider them incapable of such great glory, or perhaps not yet worthy of it. Immediately afterwards, they moderate their earlier venturesomeness with meek and modest restraint, saying in the bride's presence: 'What is your beloved?' Clearly they are submitting their desires wholly to her discretion, leaving it to her to fulfill them in accordance with their small capacity and her personal judgement.

On the other hand, in these previous words of theirs it must also be carefully noted that they do not say: 'What is your beloved more than the Father', or 'more than that eternal generation of his,' or

anything of this kind, but 'What is your
beloved more than another beloved?' It is
evident that their thirst is to draw something sweetly to themselves from the very
fount of love, rather than argue boldly
about the generation of the Word. It is as if
they say: let our mother not reckon us
among the daughters of Belial, occupying
ourselves with things too great and marvels
beyond us.* We are content with our small           *Ps 131:1
measure, we do not reach above our grasp.
We keep within the bounds of your master's school, within the confines of your
holy discipline. Let others probe into the
sacred mystery of divine generation,
reverenced even by the angels. Let them
enter the depths of judgement and there
boldly penetrate and bring into the open
what is sealed in the treasure-houses of
God. At all events, let those who think
they are thus taking the kingdom of
heaven by force beware! It may well be that
they will be considered intruders to be
overwhelmed by its glory rather than received into it! Let them see for themselves
how rashly they presume, and for what
end. It is all too obvious that by an impudent disputation like this, modesty is driven
away, reverence for majesty is weakened
and the curb-rein of the fear of God is
relaxed. If charity, the end of the whole
law, does not completely die, it is certainly gravely undermined by these con-
tentious rivalries. Moses did not lightly
rush forward to the sight of God. He was
called twice, he took off his shoes as a

*Cf. Ex 3:5*

penitent, and he went forward in fear and trembling. And he did not yet dare, even thus, to look directly at the Lord.* We find the same thing with Elijah. When he had hidden in his cave from the sight of the power of the Lord and he was called by God by name, he covered his face with his

*1 K 19:13*

cloak.* Here we have men of great sublimity, and yet what lowliness, what a fitting reverence, what a heavy weight of dread beneath the lofty peak of majesty! On this matter no more need be said.

2. Well then, to return to the daughters of Jerusalem, how much we can draw from these words of theirs! At the moment their whole desire, the real point of their two-fold query, is that those who thirst may receive what they crave from the hand of the bride. Let her draw either from the font, which is in Jerusalem, or from the

*Cf. 1 Ch 11:17*

cistern, which is in Bethlehem;* it is for her to choose. It is also for her to distribute in proportion as the spirit of charity gives her to speak, measuring out in her hand and sharing among them as she wishes. For the spouse is two-fold in the nobility of his nature, and in both he is as wonderfully renowned as he is beautiful and lovable beyond all conceiving. The daughters fix their eyes upon the bride, so that from her breasts either wine or milk may flow out to them, or, as a crowning grace, wine and milk together.

The bride hastens to meet desires so sweetly conceived by the spirit of charity, desires giving birth as well to charity, though not without pain and grief. For here, in all truth, are pains like those of child-birth, until the charity of Christ is fully formed and they can say: 'As we have heard, so likewise have we seen.'* Mean- *Cf. Ps 48:8 while, whoever is a bride of the Lord, whoever is a mother of Jesus, groans in sympathy with anyone groaning, and gives birth with her, and stands by her in her delivery. And when at last she has given birth, she ardently rejoices with her because a child is born into the world.* It seems to *Jn 16:21 her that she herself brought forth the child, and she cries out: 'To us a child is born, to us a son is given!'* Surely, in days *Is 9:6 gone by, Mary was deeply moved by feel- ings like this when she went up with haste into the hills and from the sanctuary of God, her own heart, greeted Elizabeth, who was pregnant by God's grace.* Day *Cf. Lk 1:39 uttered speech to day.† She met her with †Ps 19:2 blessings of sweetness,* she took on the *Cf. Ps 21:4 duty of a midwife and she turned the pangs of labor to a fruitful joy. For from that utterance of hers, fragrant beyond telling, it came about that John as well as Elizabeth drew in the inestimable sweetness of the perfume. What a good and careful mid- wife, who forestalled with such inexpress- ible happiness the approaching birth-pangs of the mother and in addition the tears of the expectant baby as well! It was not only the womb of Elizabeth that she satisfied, but also the fruit of her womb. It was surely Jesus who opened her hand and filled everything with goodness,* baptizing *Cf. Ps 104:28

mother and son in the Holy Spirit.

So it is that the bride of the Lord comes quickly now to meet the daughters of Jerusalem. They are pregnant with the Holy Spirit and they await their lady's return from the wedding feast. She girds herself and makes them sit down,* providing for them as her beloved provided for her, telling them what her God has said to her. In a word, she places before them the kind of things the Lord placed before her when she returned from the wedding feast. She says therefore: 'My beloved is all radiant and ruddy.'* 'You want to know, o daughters of Jerusalem,' she adds, 'in what way my beloved is more than another beloved. A vast theme from every angle! My beloved is all radiant and ruddy. If you want to understand, my beloved is a fire that shines and burns, especially because of his beloved Father, since he too is a fire, and a font of light and heat to his only Son, my beloved. For the Father loves his Son, my beloved, and he loves him with a love as marvellous as it is beyond our comprehending. He has poured into him all the fulness of his glory and power. So great is the force of love pouring out on him from that font of love that the Father and his beloved Son, my beloved, are not only coeternal and coequal with each other, but they have also one and the same essence, in every way undifferentiated. Therefore this font of love is the primary channel of living water, a font of life to all who drink from it. All holy love draws its

*Lk 12:37

*Sg 5:10

joy from this font, and in order that it may perpetually flow towards eternal life, from which also it must spring, it wells up forever with desire towards its font, rushing tirelessly back to its origin. So great is the power of this love which flows from the very deepest and primary font of love that it unites its lover to its source. However, there is no question of unity of nature, for that is something unique and incomparable that is possible only in the source itself. What we do have here is a personal cleaving in an indissoluble bond of union. For the man who cleaves to the Lord, becomes one spirit with him.* *1 Co 6:17*

3. 'When you ask, then, how my beloved is more than another beloved, I have a ready answer at hand. In the same way as the Father is lovely and desirable, just so is his only-begotten Son. Radiant from the radiant, red from the ruddy. Seeing that my beloved is truly a fire, he shines and burns exceedingly. But he does this as one whom the Father loves and he is in turn loved totally with an equal charity, for the Father is the source of light and heat to his loved and loving only Son. So together they are one light and one heat, and light as being wisdom, truth, holiness, goodness. Wisdom, the artificer of all things, having all knowledge. Truth, vanquishing with its brightness the shadows of error, the lurking-places of deceit. Holiness, intolerant of all corruption and impurity. Goodness, freely communicating its very self, even to the unworthy. Look well then

at the likeness to these things in our
visible light, about which Light itself said:

*Gn 1:3

"Let there be light," and there was light.*
In a certain manner of its own, that light
also illumines the blind and teaches man
wisdom, stripping away the darkness of
blindness and ignorance in which night had
overwhelmed and enveloped him. By the
sudden dazzling of its brightness it drives
darkness away and lays bare its works,
showing up all their falsity. Into that light

*Ws 7:23

nothing defiled gains entrance*, but it has
kept itself immaculate. Finally, it shines
equally on the good and the bad, and gives
itself freely to both. O most beautiful
Light, o radiance of light eternal, you were
like that from the beginning, you were
like that, o everlasting loveliness, in those
everlasting days of yours, in the years of
your eternity! You were like that, o Lord
Jesus, wise, true, holy, good, but you were
this for yourself and for your beloved
Father, who loves you. With you was the

*Ps 110:3

beginning on the day of your birth,* and
you were with him, and you were total joy
to him, and so was he to you.'

4. Still, as you were not only light from

*Jn 1:5

light,* but also the font of brightness, you
wanted to reveal this great good and to
share it with your creatures. All of a sudden, then, you glowed radiantly forth in
those whom you chose as sharers in so
great a good. You called the stars, and they

*Ba 3:34

answered, 'Here we are.'* And they shone
forth to you with gladness, eternally de-
lighting in you, their incommunicable good,

perpetually and gloriously sparkling in you, their source. But when it comes to us, whom you created to delight in you, we have turned away, wanting to keep our strength to ourself alone, and we have blundered into the darkness of ignorance and weakness. It was a night of utter blackness, so much so that we did not remember you or from where we first fell or where in the end we would land. Worse still, there was not in us even any awareness of having fallen and of yet rushing headlong down. Then, too, o true light, in all this darkness of ours, then you shone, but our darkness did not comprehend you.* You were close, *Jn 1:5* you who are never distant, but we were distant, we were far away from you. We were living in banishment, in a country very distant from your light, in the country of the shadow of death. You were inaccessible to us, because in your regard it is useless to rise up early.* In your regard *Ps 127:21* every effort of virtue, however great, is completely futile and vain, unless the light of your grace goes before it.

5. We were wholly unable to come near to you, the dawning splendor of light eternal, and yet you came near to us by that same free and innate goodness with which, born from the Father's womb before the daystar,* you glimmered so won- *Ps 110:3* derfully in the saints' first splendors. Since you were wisdom, the fashioner of all things,* with wonderful and delicate craft *Ws 7:22* you have fashioned a salvation adapted to the blind and sickly. The world did not

have the wisdom to know you in the invisible light of your wisdom, so it seemed proper to your honor to enlighten the blind and to cure the sick by means of a foolishness. You were a great light hidden in the bosom of your Father; you came forth from your retreat into our market-place. You became a great light for the great, and a small lamp for the little ones; you became a lamp not only visible to our eyes but palpable to our touch. In this way you brought news of it to your friend, that it was for him to possess and mount up to it. You broke forth from the pure womb of the virgin, o purest of lights, and there indeed you set your tabernacle in the sun,* but one which you fashioned for yourself as the font of light. Therefore, o blessed light, since you were wisdom, wisely you subdued yourself to the unwise.

*Ps 19:4

Further, because you were truth, you threw your beams into the darkness to dispel the night of our ignorance and to refute the works of darkness. You thundered from the cloud of the flesh, threatening judgement and announcing the kingdom. You glittered in signs and wonders and made it clear that you were our true and sole salvation, taking away our sin. Yet it would have been useless for you to show these things to us exteriorly, had you not also shone interiorly. Since you were holiness, you took great delight in showing your mercy towards us. You filled us with your fear, through which you make us holy, turning us away from our darkness and drawing us compassionately to you, the true light. And finally, since you were goodness, so that you might garb in honor those who had put on the livery of confession, and we might walk becomingly as in the day,* you wrapped us around in the light of your justice. You gave us goodness, infusing the spirit of your grace, and our earth has given its fruit.*

*Rm 13:13*

*Ps 85:2*

And so, o sweet light, o life-giving light, by sending forth your wisdom and truth you instructed our mind; by instilling the light of your holiness and goodness you wonderfully illuminated our heart. In these wonderful ways your lightning has lit up the world,* just as you light up every single son of light in the world. This is what can be said about the radiance of the eternal light, that is, the radiance of the beloved, as far as we can understand it, or rather, as far as he gives us to understand.

*Ps 77:18*

6.  Now let us hear about the redness of the true fire, He himself is this fire, too, in that he himself has given it. For what Isaiah says cannot rightly be applied to any other than the beloved: 'The light of Israel will become a fire, and his holy one a flame.* If we then look closely at the qualities of this material fire, [we see that] it separates and purifies, it burns up and consumes, it melts and unites, it changes into its own nature and transforms. All this is true of the holy one of Israel, the only begotten of the Most High, to whom the Father has entrusted all judgement. He will fully and visibly accomplish this justice at the end of

*Is 10:17*

time, but even now, in a not-invisible manner, he does not cease to perform it,
judging and separating a holy people out
from an unholy, refining by heat into
purity the dross of his silver. It is not so
much that he himself takes his seat as judge
to kindle a fire, but what is much more
effective, he himself is the fire, kindling to
purify the sons of Levi.

Seize upon me now, Lord, in the present
day, before you come at the day of your
wrath! Seize upon me, not in your wrath,
but as you seized upon the sons of Levi and
as you reproved the daughters of Jerusalem,
in a spirit of judgement and a spirit of
flame! Renew both these spirits within my
heart, so that standing before you at your
tribunal, I myself may both judge myself
justly and punish myself severely. For who
will stay erect when they see you? Such is
your dread, who will even be able to think
of the day of your coming, when you come
as a burning and consuming fire? O dread
and terrible judge, what strength, though
of stone, what flesh, though of bronze, will
be able on that day to withstand your
face, burning with zeal and deeply flushed
with wrath? You will be wrapped in a
mantle of zeal, as of one taking vengeance,
and you will hold in your hand your flash-
ing sword and the other instruments of
your wrath! O the many judgments of the
abyss of God! How truly wise and blessed is
he who carefully lays up these judgments
for himself in the secret of his heart! He has
put the abyss into treasure chests, so as to

store for himself in them an incomparable treasure, fearing the terror of the Lord now, and so he need not fear it hereafter.

7. As we have said already, our God is a fire burning up and consuming, but he is also one that melts and unites. To this there is no witness more faithful and trustworthy than she who has tested it by experience. She can say from her own knowledge: 'My soul melted when my beloved spoke.'* Who has melted the soul of his beloved if not he who is fire? Who will give us of that fire, very fierce yet very gentle, which is under the wings of the cherubim and blazes eternally on your heavenly altars, my king and my God? Who will at least give each of us one single living and life-giving ember, inflaming and melting? In the presence of this fire may my heart become like melting wax!* May my soul faint away before your salvation, Lord,* may all of me faint, even my eyes, so that it is no longer I that live, but Christ who lives in me!* This fire melts in order to recreate, dissolves in order to unite. With the girdle of eager charity and the cord of unbreakable peace it unites God to the soul and the soul to God. For he who abides in love abides in God, and God in him.*

Finally, we await in patience the day when our blessed regeneration will be accomplished, when that most powerful fire will transform and change us into himself. For we have a sure and most trustworthy promise, that our mortal and corruptible nature will be absorbed by

*Sg 5:6

*Cf. Ps 22:14

*Cf. Ps 119:81

*Ga 2:20

*1 Jn 4:16

glory and our body be made like to the
brightness of Christ's body. Furthermore,
what is going to happen with respect to the
likeness of God? Who will dare to speak of
these ineffable things, who will dare to
compute or convey with a human understanding what exceeds all understanding?
In short, if iron thrust into the fire is
engulfed by its mighty force and takes on a
fiery heat and color, how Christ will
triumph on the day of his glory, when he
ascends on high, joyfully taking captive to
himself the whole of mankind! On that
day and throughout eternity, he alone
will be wonderful and glorious in his saints.
O vestment upon vestment, panoply of
eternal light, for whom has God prepared
you, who will be found worthy to be clad
in you? But why are you cast down, my
soul, and why do you groan within me?*
Keep your hope high, for the Lord is good
to those who hope in him.* Act with confidence, hold in your bosom a blessed hope
for yourself, or, what will surely be much
better and safer, place it in God, who alone
is strong to guard what you entrust to him.*

*\*Ps 43:5*

*\*Lm 3:25*

*\*2 Tm 1:12*

*Therefore, o Father of mercies, receive,
I beg, what we entrust to you, the hope of
blessedness which you promised us. Give it
back to us on the day when your glory is
revealed, for the sake of him whom you
love and in whom your soul is well pleased,
your blessed Son, Jesus Christ our Lord,
who with you and the Holy Spirit
lives and reigns, God for ever
and ever.
Amen.*

## SERMON EIGHT

*The beginning of the eighth sermon.* Of the
fourfold radiance of holiness in Christ, of
which the first is the perfect innocence of
the flesh, the second the utter wisdom and
perfect justice of the soul, the third the
taking up of that man into God, the fourth
the restraint of that man's humility in the
face of such great majesty.

I F I AM IRKSOME to you, while
putting forth every effort to be helpful, I am sorry. But I want my soul to
take heart from the Love of the Word of
God and from the burning eloquence of
this love song, and as often as I turn away
from it for a space, my soul usually
becomes like a leather bag in the frost!*      *Cf. Ps 119:83
So I have indulged myself a little in this
restful labor, hoping that you will profit, if
you desire it. It is not a slight task to gather
sticks from here and there, to arrange the
sticks in a pile and, by dint of blowing, to
coax a fire from a small spark. Yet if the
result of all this work is that you are willing
and eager to warm yourselves with me at
the hearth of your little spark, then I
rejoice at the word of the Lord, like one
that finds great spoil.* But if you withdraw     *Ps 119:6
from approaching this little fire of ours

161

because you know of one larger and more
blissful, then I will keep my fire in my
bosom. Perhaps, shut up within my bones
it may blaze more fiercely and make my
heart glow within me, so that in my
meditation a fire may burn bright.* If you
prefer not to listen to me, I will sing to my
beloved with Isaiah,* since I do not dare to
do so with the bride.

*Cf. Is 5:1*

Meanwhile, I will try to mingle with the
daughters of Jerusalem and listen in silence
to the voice of the bride as she proceeds
from the marriage chamber. She not only
speaks the things of love, she brings them
into existence; and by listening to her I become fit to hear the voice of the spouse.
You are also daughters of Jerusalem. Is not
the bride herself your mother, who brought
you forth and gave you birth, who dandled
you on her knees and fed you from her
breasts? Is she not herself the cause of your
joy, the goal of your journey, the height of
your desire? What use are your tongue and
ear, unless the voice of the spouse and the
voice of the bride sound on your tongue and
ring in your ear? He who is of the earth
speaks of the earth,* and godless men
relate rumors to one another.† But to us let
words of God be as sweet as they really
are, sweeter than honey and the honey-
comb.*

*Jn 3:31*
†*Ps 119:85*

*Ps 19:10*

2.  So, while the maidens seek repeatedly
to find out from the bride in what way her
beloved is more than another beloved, she
herself meets both parts of the question
with this brief response: 'My beloved is all

radiant and ruddy.' What appertains to the glory which the spouse has eternally from his Father, I tried to explain in the previous sermon, as far as he enabled me. It still remains, likewise by his favor, to expatiate on that same reply, but with reference to the glory of his beauty as son of man, fairest among the sons of men.*   *Ps 45:2

In fact the lovely splendor of his radiance and redness make him most exceedingly admirable and amiable. He nourishes the soul, which gazes on him with complete satisfaction. The flesh of Jesus is food indeed, and his blood is drink indeed,* for   *Jn 6:55
those who have thoroughly ruminated on the inexpressible charity and humility of his incarnation and passion. They know how to draw it down through healthy and hungry throats to the depths of their bowels. Happy are those eaglets who, on assuming their wings, soar straight to the body of Christ, and with an insatiable hunger—let me not call it a voracious maw—devour his flesh and lap his blood! Yet why should I scruple to say voracious maw, when the law lays it down as part of the ceremony of this meal that the flesh of the lamb be eaten hastily, that is, voraciously, and the head be consumed together with the entrails?* What else, think you, is this   *Cf. Ex 12:3-11
intense voracity in consuming the lamb but a mysterious ardor to see the incarnate God? I put it to you, what else is that voracity if not a certain sweet hunger and hungry sweetness, as it were tasting in advance, sacramentally, the first fruits of the incar-

nation and passion of Christ, and stretching out with utter longing to the fulness? And let us, too, if we are not to be degenerate fledglings, let us hasten with all strength of wing and vision to consume and to drain that noble eagle. Let us clutch our prey with beak and claw and cling to him tenaciously.

3. Well then, let us look at the radiance and redness of the beloved, according to the glory of the humanity he assumed. At the moment, four qualities of that lovely radiance come to mind, and each one of them exceeds all grasp of human or angelic comprehension. The first is the complete innocence and perfect sanctity of that most holy flesh. The second is the complete wisdom and perfect justice of that most exalted soul. The third is the glorious assumtion of that man into God. The fourth is the wonderful restraint of his humility under the load of such great glory. Who is fit even to consider these things, let alone to expound them? If we cannot conceive them in our words, let us at least bring them to birth in our delight in them.

4. How pure and radiant was that flesh, brought forth by the virgin, conceived by the Holy Spirit! The glory of his holiness was inherited from his mother as well as from the Holy Spirit, and so it was inviolable it itself besides giving health to the whole stock. In the past, a foolish woman, Eve, poured out the leaven of concupiscence into the mass of human

nature, and by that very act made this leaven an hereditary and inescapable necessity. So likewise, through some new and miraculously unchanged law, the wisest of virgins poured straight into her son, as his natural inheritance, the leaven of innocence and sanctity, by the wisdom and power of the Holy Spirit. If blessed Job could say that compassion took root in him from the beginning and piety issued forth from his mother's womb,* and the apostle maintained that Timothy had to some extent inherited the grace of faith, first from his grandmother Lois, and then from his mother Eunice,* then how much more is that which was born of the spotless flesh of the virgin, through the working of the Holy Spirit, unable to be anything but virginal and free from all corruption.

*Cf. Jb 31:18

*Cf. 2 Tm 1:5

The disease of original sin was not able wholly to infect and poison human nature. It stops short at destroying in the bodies of new-born infants the tiny flower of virginity, though frail indeed and weak. In actuality, everyone, even if conceived in sin, is born a virgin. How much more, then, does virginal conception, followed by virginal child-birth, make hereditary the splendor of holiness! This is not the inheritance of corruptible innocence that we spoke of above, but an unfading inheritance of angelic purity. Let me add, that if, by the kindness of our creator, that original mark was so deeply imprinted in our first parents that it was too strong to be uprooted from deep in the flesh by any subsequent

appearance of sons or grandsons (whether
of their own parentage or, afterwards, of
others) to a far greater extent the virgin
Mary had the power to pass on an inheritance to her child! We believe that in her,
through the overshadowing power of the
most High, human nature flowered again
to spotless innocence. I am not saying that
in her the heat of bodily concupiscence was
tamed and lulled to rest, I am saying that
to her very depths it was killed and buried,
so that the glory of virginal honor, which
she herself received as a free gift, she
transmitted by hereditary to her offspring.
There is this point, too. All christian
piety, without any agitation or disagree-
ment, is of the one opinion, that if the
first stock of our race had remained pure,
original justice and inviolable innocence
would have descended to their posterity
by the law of inheritance. Why then should
she, who once more renewed the ancient
privilege, yes, and in a far more excellent
manner, why should she be deprived of at
least the normal privilege, as it should
have been?

I may have spoken rather fully on this
point, because I hear that some of you are
disturbed by the remark I made about the
Lord Jesus having inherited innocence from
his virgin mother. If anyone thinks this is a
novelty, and as such impious, I do not
want so to defend words that I offend
charity. Still, whoever feels like this, let
him quietly read to himself what Anselm
thought about this when treating of the

virginal conception,† what that orthodox and, to say the least, most learned man from Igny,* or any of the holy fathers thought. For myself, though, I prefer rather the riches of loving concord than those of the intellect, and, as the wise man says, I feel it better to yield to another than be the slave of contention.

The blessed mother of God fashioned a garment for the sole beloved fruit of her womb, and the Holy Spirit wove it with her.† It was a garment woven throughout from above,* a garment of incomparable whiteness, such as before or after has never been seen on earth, a garment which no spot can bespatter or hand impair. This is the kingly garment which alone the King of kings has worn from his very beginning. Without a doubt it has written on it this inscription: King of kings and Lord of Lords.* This is a privilege reserved solely for the mother who bore him,† a privilege reserved solely for the flesh of him so born. Before that day, what stone had been cut out of the mountain without human hand,* what stone will next be cut? It was fitting that the gate of virginity be kept shut for the prince alone. He alone should be found there, as the one to whom that gate lay open in conception and future birth. O princely, noble, great-hearted bud, I do not know whether it is with more truth or kindness that you said to your beloved: 'I am the flower of the field.'† You are quite truly a flower, beautiful to behold, smooth to touch, sweet to

†Cur Deus Homo
II, 16; PL 158:
416-19; ed.
Schmitt 2:119,
and De conceptu
virginali 20; PL
158:425;
Schmitt 2:160

*Guerric,
S. in ann. beatae
Mariae 2,1;
PL 185:120;
CF 32:39-40.

†Cf. Lk 1:35
*Jn 19:23

*1 Tm 6:15
†A phrase from the
Ms is here missing
from the printed
text, which, after
the quotation
should read:
'singulare privi-
legium matri
huic sic gigendi',
before going on to
'singulare privi-
legium etiam'.

*Dn 2:34

†Sg 2:1

smell, bringing forth the fruit of eternal salvation for all who see you, touch you, smell you. You took away from your field its thorn and bramble, you removed the reproach of neglect and the curse of sterility. In a word, you blessed your land,* and you blessed your field with all the riches of fertility, sweetness and beauty.

5. And now, what can I say worthy of the soul of Jesus, which was the mediator and made the bond in that unspeakable union by which human flesh was united to the Word of God? In that soul are hid all the treasures of wisdom and knowledge,* in it are stored all the riches of God's judgements so fully and immeasurably that nothing can be added and nothing taken away. In this soul the liberty of the human will, in the full dignity of its freedom, was restored to the integrity of the ancient decree, completely and peacefully, forever after to be enjoyed by a perpetual decree. In the volume of the book it is thus written of him;* it is thus written and stamped with the seal of the king, it is inscribed by the right hand of the whole Trinity. It is no longer permissible to break the seal or contrive anything in secret against the inscriber or the inscription. From now on it belongs to this soul alone to hear with joy what the burglar hears with grief: 'You are the seal of perfection, full of wisdom and perfect in beauty.'* Among all the creatures of God, there is nothing and can be nothing more like God than this soul, nothing equally like.

*Col 2:3

*Ps 40:7-8

*Ezk 28:12

Whoever desires to be reformed to the likeness of God from defilement by the enemy,
let him take counsel with that soul. The
seal is in his power and the writing case is at
his side.*                                          *Ezk 9:2*

6. Up to now my soul has cleaved to
paved ground. Oh, if only it would now
cleave to you, o chosen, o precious soul of
the chosen one! With you to pity it, it is
not completely bare. In your eyes, I cover
my nakedness as best I can, with old rags
somehow stitched together by a constant
plying of the needle of repentance. But
your cloak is very large, wide enough to
cover us both. Stretch it out over this poor
little soul of mine! Certainly my justice is
like a garment that the moths have eaten,*          *Jb 13:28*
but your justice is like a mantle of light, a
tunic without seam. There is no way in
which it can be torn or ripped, and there is
equally no way in which it can be stitched
together or patched. So I will wrap myself
in it with perfect confidence. It has come
to me from heaven, falling to my lot as one
who has complete belief in him who
justifies the ungodly.* If you are to judge            *Rm 4:5*
me, o my Lord, if the Father has really put
all judgement into your hands, then see
how your justice, by your free gift, is my
justice! I will remember only that, and
throwing myself onto it, I will not be
ashamed. And so, if you judge me, then
judge me according to this justice that is
in me.* With that to cover me, I will not          *Ps 7:8*
fear when winter comes, or the heat of
summer. Instead, I will glory, because the

*Is 61:10

Lord has clothed me with the garment of
salvation, has covered me with the robe of
righteousness.*

7.  Consider with me, if you can, if it admits of being considered, what a great peace
has arisen in the days of this king, what a
great exultation and, finally, what a great
glory has forthwith spread throughout our
boundaries. At the first moment of his
coming the whole law of sin fell silent, all
murmur ceased of the flesh against the
spirit and the spirit against the flesh. What
joy there was in the soul of this peaceful
king of ours, flowing from the peace he had
beneath him, the justice he had within
him, the glory of God he had above him!
Very many things come to mind about the
glory of that ineffable union, wonderful
things, but I can say little that will be
worthy.

First of all, I admit not knowing whether
to wonder more at the dignity of the
assumed nature or the dignity of the man
who assumed it. But let us bless the Lord
our God, Father, Son and Holy Spirit, for
having done so for us, by loving mutual
agreement! They have done for us as they
arranged together. They have not only
made man to their own image and like-
*Gn 5:3
ness,* but they have made a man who is
their own image and likeness, something
no man has dared desire or hope for.
Blessed be the Holy Trinity and undivided
Unity! Calling together their friends and
neighbors, with the ineffable delight of
love they have made to them this

announcement: 'Rejoice with me and congratulate Adam, because now, behold, "Adam has become like one of us!" '* O with what great joy this was announced! With what great jubilation it was welcomed throughout that country! O with what great exultation it presently resounded in our land, and yet with what great grief of gnawing envy it thundered in an enemy land, in the ears of Assyria!

*Gn 3:22*

On that day the Lord rescued my soul from the hand of Assyria, who had afflicted me without any reason and, hurling me from my place, had made me sit in darkness like those long dead.* The proud and wicked had striven after the place of the only Begotten, that is, likeness to the most High. He fell down, not only from that hope, but from the place which had been his before, as was just. He passed by without hindrance as far as I was concerned, yet he envied me the place which had fallen to me by lot, though I had neither done nor wished him any harm. What more is there to say? He promised me the treasures of knowledge, the riches of immortality, and finally, likeness to God. And so I went away because of the advice of the wicked, dragged away and seduced—though that is no excuse. Immediately I learned by experience who it was who had deceived me, and that God is truthful and he, on the contrary, deceitful. As a result, I have borne the wrath of God from that day unto this, the time of our God's good pleasure. Now the Son of David has come to sit upon his

*Ps 143:3*

throne and to render judgement to him
who suffers wrong. If you want to know,
then this is the judgement: I was cast down
by one's attack, I am also raised up by the
other's hand. I had done nothing sinful
against my attacker that I should be cast
down, for Assyria accused me without
cause.* Likewise, I was saved freely and
without cause. It was not for any justice
of mine that the Lord rescued me.

*Cf. Is 52:4*

8. It was only envy that drove my
enemy to throw me down, only compassion that drew my rescuer to lift me up.
The one, falling headlong from heaven,
overwhelmed me with the bulk of his greatness, the deceit of his cunning, the force of
his strength. My rescuer, coming gently
down from heaven, healed me with the
skill of his remedies, for he assumed my
flesh and bore my infirmities. I had made a
pact with hell when I offered myself to him
for sale, but because I did it without the
knowledge of my Lord, and we were both
making an agreement to his harm, my
Lord came down from heaven to seek his
servant. He sat on his throne of judgement
and dissolved our pact, for we had settled
upon it craftily and wickedly, and it was
much against him as against me. In short, he
took the bond from the accuser's hand and
snatched the yoke of the oppressor from
my shoulder, and from then on he imposed
on me his own sweet yoke.

It was nevertheless declared that whatever
I had been falsely promised should be fulfilled, so as to confound the lie and its father.

Hell promised immortality, he promised the riches of knowledge, he promised, too, a likeness to God. The Lord judged the cause of the poor, and granted all these things. Hell changed the truth of God into lies, for he said: 'You shall not die,' whereas God had said: 'You shall die.'* So God, whose *Cf. Gn 3:3* nature is goodness, turned his evil to good purposes, and at the right time, changed his lie to truth. Seeing and hearing this, how angry the Evil One will be, how he will gnash his teeth and pine away!* Yet *Cf. Ps 112:10* there is a wound more deadly still, which the rival of mankind is quite unable to endure. For the place which in his rash arrogance he coveted, God with indescribable goodness has awarded to me, for he has awarded it to my Lord. For the Lord said to my Lord, you are my Son, sit at my right hand.* *Ps 110:1*

All this has been said in respect of the dignity of the man who was gloriously assumed into God.

9. The sheer dignity of the Person who assumed this flesh and his full wonder will shine out all the more brightly from a comparison with the pride and blasphemy of Assyria. For he thought and uttered evil against the Most High, saying to the woman: 'God knows that on whatever day you eat of this tree, your eyes will be opened and you will be as gods.'* Mark the impudent *Gn 3:5* blasphemy, hurling into the face of the Creator the brand of falsehood, envy and pride! Therefore God sent his Son to free him from these accusations and provide

every conscience with what is very honorable, not only in the sight of God, but even
in the sight of men.* In defence of the *2 Co 8:21
truth, even though he himself should be
silent, death itself, which has reigned from
the time of Adam and will go on reigning
up to the last day, death, too, cries out and
fights on his behalf. All envy shrinks away
from his, far from his thoughts, for the
goodness and loving kindness of our Savior
has appeared.* He freely gives us his Son *Tt 3:4
and all that is his together with him, and in
turn he communicates to him all that
is ours.

Very sure are the decrees* of the divine *Ps 92:5
humility, the stooping down of majesty,
the taking up of human nature, the emptying out of wisdom and strength. To see
how bright and appealing this is, let us
compare it with the swollen mass of pride
in the boastful heart of Assyria. For he
said: 'I will ascend to heaven, above the
stars of God I will set my throne on high.'* *Is 14:13
Let the Son of God answer him: 'I will
descend from heaven, and I will be less
than the angels.' The one says: 'I will
ascend above the heights of the clouds,
I will make myself like the Most High.'* *Is 14:14
The other said: 'I will descend even to the
likeness of man and be reckoned as one of
those who go down into the pit'.* Truly, *Ps 87:4
Lord, your works are great, fashioned to
your every desire!* The rival of my salva- *Cf. Ps 111:2
tion and your glory you have terribly confounded; me, your poor servant, you have
mercifully and marvelously saved. You

have saved your holy name, you have freed it from all suspicion, and you have added to it new glory, above all its former renown.

10. We have now three kinds of radiance pertaining to glory in Christ Jesus: that of the flesh, that of the soul, and that of the blessed union with the Word of God. There remains still a fourth, the marvellous humility with which that man bore the weight of such glory. But the shortness of time holds me back and, still more, a fear of wearying and overburdening you. Most of all, the dignity of the subject itself is a deterrent, for it cannot easily endure constriction within the brief limits of this page. So, by God's providence, it will have a time reserved for itself. Then your throats will be keener through hunger for the word of God, and you will be more eager to receive the bread itself, all fresh and warm, as if just taken from the oven. May the Lord Jesus open his hand and give it to you through this hand of mine, he who lives and reigns with God the Father and the Holy Spirit, one God,
for ever and ever.
Amen.

## SERMON NINE

*The beginning of the ninth sermon.* Of the virtue of humility, great in all the just, and especially outstanding in Christ. Of the two kinds of humility in Christ, namely, the exterior, under five heads, signified by the five stones from the brook, and then the interior, under the three heads of fear, obedience and holy thanksgiving.

TODAY we have before us a sermon on the humility of the beloved. May he himself help us to treat it worthily and with reverence. On the occasion when we spoke about the radiant whiteness of the beloved, it so happened that we gave fourth place to humility, placing on its shoulders the weight of all the glory of that threefold radiance we discussed previously. The weight of that glory is a huge weight, weight upon weight, but humility is enormously strong. She rejoices to load it on her shoulder, and the Lord of hosts is with her.

With good reason we termed radiance that which is not only most radiantly white itself, but has also the power of restoring to utter whiteness the most absolute blackness. Let one who has experienced this bear witness: 'You will sprinkle me with hyssop and I shall be clean, you will wash me and I shall be whiter than snow.'* Although humility is certainly a daughter of the king, shining out among the other daughters with incomparable beauty, she has been chosen for a special office. It is her lot to clean the dust from the feet of the daughters of Jerusalem, to make them all pure,* to bathe the feet of the saints, to wash their garments, to hold them out to the sunlight, and so, in the end, to restore them radiantly white to those who hasten to the marriage of the bridegroom and the bride. Do not be surprised at this. She has received from her Father the power to baptize afresh the most wicked and the most lost, who have completely lost their baptismal purity. She clothes them in the first robe and puts a ring on their finger and shoes on their feet.* She has, of course, a vast throng of handmaids assisting her in these tasks, and for a washbowl she has a huge sea, great and wide. The waters of the deep abyss make it seethe and foam, spreading out to wash sinners and the unclean.* And the water of this washbowl is a mingling of three streams: the sweet waters of the mercies of the Lord, which are for ever,* the bitter waters of penitential tears, and the blood of the new testament, the precious blood, the blood of Jesus. So in this washbowl the daughter of the king shows new signs and works further wonders.* Namaan loses his leprosy, the Ethiopian changes his skin and

*Ps 51:7

*Cf. Is 4:4

*Lk 15:22

*Cf. Zc 13:1

*Si 36:6

the leopard his spots,* the just become juster still, and the saintly more sanctified.*

Hearing often these wonderful and marvellous things about the beauty of the king's daughter and her outstanding virtue, I, too, in all my wretchedness have desired her beauty. Whenever I look at her and see her lovely grace, I am deeply moved. I burn with love-longing and I seek to take her to myself as a bride. Scarcely has the flame of love seized hold of me than I have sent an embassy to my Lord, the king her Father, to press him with prayers, entreaties, sighs and tears to give her to me freely, out of his overflowing goodness. But it goes hard with a poor man like myself! Up to now my prayers go unanswered, and it is only she herself who keeps my hope alive. I own so very little, and it would be a great thing for me to become son-in-law to a king.* Yet I cherish a great hope of finally attaining my desire, partly from the liberality of the Father, who approves my petition, encourages my prayer and promises an answer—provided that in the end I serve him as a recompense for her—and partly from the sheer goodness of the king's daughter. She graciously anticipates those who long for her, and has sometimes, though secretly and swiftly, admitted me to her desired embrace.

If this royal maiden has such power in the remotest borders of her Father's kingdom, how much more she wields in the actual palace of the king, whose price no man knows,* except its own inmates and

*Cf. Jr 13:23
*Rv 22:11

*Cf. 1 S 18:22

*Jb 28:13

servants. So it is to the only Son of God, the firstborn of the Father, the mediator between God and men that she gives herself completely. To him she wholly displays her power and pours forth her beauty without reserve. His glory is twofold, one within and one without. For even if all his glory is from within,* it is not all wholly within, since a great part of it shines forth outwardly. The fulness of both rests upon him to whom God has given the Spirit without measure. One humility is in the sentiments of the heart, the other in external actions, but he has received both in their fulness, being full of grace and truth. For, who is as faithful in all things as my lord David, coming in and going out at the king's command?*

2.   Let us say something first about his 'going out'. He conducted himself from the very beginning with prudence and valor surpassing all the servants of the king. At your going out from your mother's womb, o my Lord David,† did you not strike the proud, overthrow the giant, and bring a mighty salvation to Israel? You proceeded against him not in the power of your arm and opposed him not in the greatness of your strength, but in our weakness, which your own hand you took from the brook of our mortality. You tucked this weakness away in your shepherd's purse, in the depths of your charity, for you came as a good shepherd to feed your people, the flock you had inherited. You took five stones from this brook, and who does not

*Ps 45:14*

*Quis in omnibus fidelis . . . — antiphon on The Magnificat from the Cistercian breviary for the Saturday before the fifth Sunday after Pentecost.*

†Cf. 1 S:17

know, o Lord my God, that these are the fivefold needs of this mortal body: hunger, thirst, nakedness, the need for shelter, the feebleness of our sickly flesh? For our sake they were mercifully taken up by your majesty, and it was through these weaknesses themselves that you so splendidly triumphed over the devil's pride. Since you were a little one, you made yourself like all little ones in weakness, except that you stood out among contemporaries of your [human] race as a more ardent seeker after littleness. You chose to be born as a stranger, and you desired to own and to inherit nothing in this world.

3. You had other stones, too, perhaps no less bright than these. There was the obligation of slavery, to which by your birth you made yourself subject, the poverty of your parents, with which you chose to contend, the meanness of the rags in which you deigned to be wrapped, the narrowness of the inn, which could not take you in—little though you were, the abasement of the manger, in which you chose to rest. Certainly these stones has little or no power in the hands of any other children, sons of Adam, and so Goliath despised them in the hands of this child, too, as if they were childish weapons. He knew nothing of this child's greatness, and how he had come with these to lay the proud low.

Look well, proud creature, at that foremost stone, the existence of privation in the Lord of majesty! In you and all the sons of pride it confounded that surging, shameless lust for mastery. The things that impose the yoke of slavery become a sublime consolation, because of humility. They are even a joy, above all for those who with consecrated heart bear the privations laid on them by voluntary slavery for Christ. Does his poverty not condemn the ostentation of riches and give a place of honor to voluntary poverty? What of the shabbiness of the rags? Do they not snuff out your glitter and render the lowly man glorious for the sake of Christ? And the constricted inn is a strong reproof to sumptious and ambitious buildings, calling us back to a measure of humility and lowliness. The abasement of the manger, too, his choice of the lowest place, how it overthrows the first seats and the ambition of those who, with such zeal, labor and expense, aspire to them!

O proud one! It was with things like these that you corrupted the whole earth. They form your two-edged sword of deceit, with which you either encourage us to joy by the promise of false good or discourage us to fear by the threat of false evil. But what a disgrace for you here! A little child, still sucking at his mother's breast, a tiny child, poor and dependent, a baby wrapped in swaddling clothes and immediately cast out of the home of his birth and flung into a manger of animals! And it is this little child who suddenly shattered your brow with a stone and hurled the sword from your hand! Even if your brow be as hard

as bronze, there is no escaping your signal
disaster, that such a very small child, with
one little stone, so quickly and easily laid
low your pride and humbled the pride of
your supporters. Sons of men, how long
will your hearts be hard,* your minds pre-   \*Ps 4:2
sumptuous? Look well at this little child
born for us, born for you, if you will have
him. Surely he destroys all excuse for our
presumption? For from his very first mo-
ments he shunned whatever gives rise to
unlawful pleasure and he opened his arms
to whatever increases holy fear.

4. O Lord my God, even if the lovers
of this world pretend not to see it and the
prince of this world takes no notice, you
have now quite certainly taken your seat
upon your throne and judged justice.*   \*Cf. Ps 9:4
With the breath of your lips you have
slain the wicked,* you have rebuked the   \*Is 11:4
manifold pride of this world in the manifold humility of your coming. Even though
you impose silence on yourself, Lord,
there is still a terrible reality in the thunder of your silence! Great and very powerful is the breath of your lips, with which
you have rebuked the proud, the greedy,
and ambitious, the lovers of ease, the seek-
ers after subtleties. You judged them by
showing in your very self the source and
model of humility, and hence you cut off
the head, that is, the source, of these vices.
The enemies of your truth, the followers of
the vanity of this world, bear on their forehead the scar of deep disgrace, for after
God emptied himself and the pride of the

*Ps 97:7*

world was overthrown by humility, they had then no further excuse for their sin. Yet they did not cast away their idols. They still cherished them and made their boast in worthless images.*

O foolish sons of men! Has the bright brilliance of the light not yet shone upon you? Do you still lie lost in sleep while such great thunder peals aloud? At the entry of the Lord into Egypt, were not the false gods of the land crushed to powder in your presence,* those false appearances of the true joy on which you had fixed your hearts? In your ears, did not the voice of majesty thunder out to worldly pride: 'Come, sit down in the dust, there is no more a throne for the daughter of the Chaldeans'?* Did there not come an answer to humility from the throne: 'Rise up from the dust, and come up higher, my beloved, for the first seat at table belongs by right to you.'* But time is pressing. For the moment this must suffice as a description of interior humility.

5.   Let us behold the entry of my God, my king, into the sanctuary.* Let us enter even into the heart of Jesus, since to that our good Master draws us. 'Learn of me,' he said, 'for I am meek and humble of heart.'* Come then, let him open to us himself that book of the new testament, the book of life, the book of wisdom, so that we may read in the heart of Jesus and be no longer disciples of men, but taught by God.* It seems to me that I see therein, traced by the finger of God, the living

*Cf. Is 91:1*

*Is 47:1*

*Cf. Lk 14:10*

*Cf. Ps 68:24*

*Mt 11:29*

*Cf. Jn 6:45*

letters of a threefold humility, and if I
could transcribe them in my own heart, I
would be truly a wise man. If you, too,
want to know them, these are the letters:
to be submissive to the divine majesty
through reverential fear, to the divine will
through obedience, to the divine glory
through thanksgiving. In all these, o Lord
Jesus, who is your equal?

6. In the silent conversation you hold
within your soul, do you not say to yourself: 'Shall my soul not be submissive to
God?* But indeed my soul will certainly          *Ps 62:1
be submissive to God.' Furthermore, if we
are treating of fear, we have the witness of
Isaiah, that 'he has filled you with the fear
of the Lord.'* It is an established fact that
among all the creatures of God, whether
on earth or in heaven, there is none who
knows more clearly than the soul of Jesus
how the majesty of the creator is to be
revered, fearfully adored, and held in highest wonder. Without the slightest doubt,
his reverence was in proportion to his
understanding. That fear is not the kind of
fear which love casts out,* like a servant          *Cf. 1 Jn 4:18
from a house, but fear more like a king's
son, loved and renowned through all his
father's house. He is honored beyond all
others in the royal palace because of the
estimable dignity of his bearing and the
awe-inspiring majesty of his countenance,
so that as he passes, all the sons of his
mother bow down before him.* Yet he          *Gn 27:29
shares a common name with that servant
whom charity cast out from the king's

house, and this is the reason: in the past, when he was a young child, he had him as a tutor, by command of the king, and he still very often obeys him in many things. Therefore queen charity takes him to her side as an inseparable companion, and decrees that she must go nowhere without him, whether to the king's wine-cellar or to his chamber. She will not even take a single step outside, whether to the garden, the vineyards, or the farm. Hence it is that the other spirits rest upon the flower from *Cf. Is 11:2* the root of Jesse,* but of this spirit it is said that he 'will fill him', and so it is fittingly named last to show it to be the governor and guardian of the others.

7. Listen then, to the obedience of Jesus: listen and marvel and imitate as far as you can. Hear how holy and righteous it was, how voluntary and dedicated, how prompt and eager, how joyful and sweet, how patient and constant, how strong and unyielding. 'I have not come,' he said, 'to do my own will, but the will of him who *Jn 6:38* sent me.'* We see its holiness and righteousness in that it has nothing of its own, but makes Jesus completely subject and surrendered to him who sent him. Again: 'I delight to do your will, my God, and your *Ps 40:8* law is in the depths of my heart.'* We see its freedom and dedication in that it knows nothing of sadness or complaint, but wholly surrenders itself into the freedom of love. Listen once more: 'My heart is ready, o *Ps 57:7* God, my heart is ready.'* We see promptness and eagerness when Jesus anticipates

his orders, and hastens forward, before he
is summoned, for whatever he must do or
suffer. Take note of that saying of his:
'My meat is to do the will of my Father,
that I may perfect his work.'* There is the $\quad$ *Jn 4:34*
joy and sweetness of obedience, which
considers itself fed when it yields and
replete when all has been fully accomplished. He said also: 'I do always the
things that please my Father.'* There is $\quad$ *Jn 8:29*
patience and constancy, in that it always
burns with the selfsame ardor. To conclude, it was said of him—and this is our
proudest boast—that: 'Christ was made
obedient to his Father even unto death,
the death of the cross.'* What is stronger $\quad$ *Ph 2:8*
than this obedience, which triumphs so
wonderfully over the Lord of hosts?

8. You have heard of the fear, you have
heard of the obedience of Jesus. Hear now
how he was given up to the glory of the
creator, how wholly poured out in thanksgiving. Rejoicing in the Holy Spirit, Jesus
said: 'I give thanks to you, Father Lord of
heaven and earth, for you have hidden
these things from the wise and prudent,
and revealed them to little ones.'* We $\quad$ *Mt 11:25*
know, too, that he is the true David, the
greatest psalmist of Israel, who raises his
voice so strongly in the psalms, with such
rejoicing and melody. This is the voice that
cries to the Father: 'I will extoll you, o
God my king, and praise your name for
ever and ever.'* This same voice cries out $\quad$ *Ps 145:1*
to all the peoples: 'Praise the Lord, all you
nations, praise him, all you peoples.'* $\quad$ *Ps 117:1*

This same voice cries to his own soul and all that is within him: 'Praise the Lord, o my soul, and let all that is within me praise his holy name.'* This same voice cries to his lute, rousing it to glorify God: 'Awake, my glory, awake, lute and lyre.'* It is no other voice that cries out to the heavenly Jerusalem: 'Praise the Lord, Jerusalem; Sion, praise your God.'* And so this same voice cries out to heaven and earth and every creature, so that everything that exists may join in praising the creator with all its might.

Hear also and, as far as you can, imitate how Jesus kept his hands and tongue completely free from any reward coming from human approval. 'The word which I speak', he said, 'I do not speak of myself. The Father who dwells in me does the work.'* And he often said: 'If I glorify myself, my glory is nothing.'* Without a doubt, blessed and to be blessed for ever is he who comes, not in his own name, but in the name of his Father. All the graces, flowing in great rivers to their fountain head, namely, the wellspring of the Father's glory, come pouring back with the selfsame power on him whom we confess and shall for all eternity confess, through his mercy. Through the one beloved Son, Jesus Christ our Lord, who with the Father and the Holy Spirit, lives and reigns, one God, for ever and ever. Amen.

*Ps 103:1

*Ps 57:8

*Ps 147:12

*Jn 14:10

*Jn 8:54

1

## SERMON TEN

*The beginning of the tenth sermon.* Of the fourfold redness of the spouse. Of his blushing for shame at the disgrace of the cross, and of the deeper and more interior blush caused by the humiliating load of our sins. How by a loving and inscrutable judgment the innocent was punished for the guilty.

AFTER THE RADIANCE of the beloved comes in its turn the redness, likewise imposing on us the burden of its praise. Yet we know and admit from the heart that we are quite unable to say or think anything worthy of it. However, here at hand is the pen of the tongue,* eager for service and waiting only for the hand of the scribe, writing busily. May he himself trim his pen to his liking, make it worthy of its purpose, fill it with the ink of his spirit. May he hold it in his own hand, move it and control it.

I take it that there are four emotions that for various reasons customarily mantle our faces with this color, and these are shame, love, anger, and joy. We believe and avow that these emotions were deep and strong in the heart of the beloved when he was still among us, and that certain of

*\*Ps 45:1*

189

them reign with him and in him, where he is now. Clearly this is true of the last three, namely, love, anger and joy. When David's heart was overflowing with a goodly theme,* and he was advancing towards the spouse, who was advancing from his bridal chamber, he met him joyfully, 'with glad shouts and songs of thanksgiving'.* He struck his lyre before the spouse and poured out his soul's rejoicing in all the strains of that holy marriage song, saying among other things: 'You have loved justice and hated wickedness, therefore God, your God, has anointed you with the oil of gladness above your fellows.'* You have already noticed, I would imagine, love in the loving of justice, wrath in the hating of wickedness, and joy in the anointing with oil.

2. But as far as his feeling of shame is concerned, it is not without a loving movement of compassion that we hear the cry of distress: 'Let not those who seek you be disgraced because of me, o God of Israel, for it is for your sake that I suffer reproach, that shame has covered my face.'* Listen, I beg you, christian soul, listen. Incline your ear with more attention. If you have in your ear, like a golden earring, any understanding of the love of Christ, listen to the words of the beloved, 'all radiant and ruddy,'* listen to what he says, what he prays in the ears of the Father. 'Let not those who seek you be disgraced because of me, o God of Israel, for it is for your sake that I suffer

*Ps 44:1

*Ps 42:4

*Ps 45:7

*Ps 69:6-7

*Sg 5:10

reproach, that shame has covered my face.'*     *Ps 69:6-7*
O fairest of the sons of men, what place is
there for this redness in that wonderful
radiance of yours, since no cause for
blushing exists or ever can exist in its
presence? Indeed, I see, I realize, and
though deeply grateful I nevertheless blush
for it, that it is on my account, o my
Lord, that you suffered this reproach, the
reproach of the cross. Though there was
absolutely nothing in you liable to shame,
even in part, yet shame covered your face,
suffusing it wholly, not in part. Take a
good look at what is set before the
beloved in this last course of his meal, not
only reproach, but reproach and shame
together. Humiliating reproach without,
rending and tormenting shame within. Reproach in the external injury to name and
body, in secret degradations as well as
open insults, in spittle, in blows, in buf-
fets, in the crowning with thorns, in the
mocking genuflections, in the flinging on
him of purple and white garments, and
finally, in the affixing to the cross and the
sharing with the wicked in every kind of
ignominy, all of which would take too long
now to recount. But to hold these things in
continual remembrance is extremely helpful and profitable towards the practice of
every virtue.

Then in a mental state of shame at the
shame which hid that face, brighter than
all light, with a red cloud of overwhelming
disgrace. Although, to be sure, he set his
face like a flint,* it is nevertheless con-     *Is 50:7*
cerning Christ Jesus inconsistent with the
dutiful exercise of faith and especially with

the insight of charity to hold that the sword did not reach into his very soul. Otherwise what is left of those words which he himself spoke in agony to his Father: 'Save me, o God, for the waters have come into my very soul'?* If a sword pierced the soul of his mother in her compassion, how much more deeply did it transpierce the soul of the Son in his passion?* And this sword is particularly two-edged and penetrating, of the bitterest grief and the vastest shame. Truly he has borne our griefs and carried our sorrows.* Thus is fulfilled what the bride said to the daughters of Jerusalem: 'My beloved is all radiant and ruddy',* when he who was so totally the flower of innocence and holiness was not only made like to sinners but reckoned among the wicked.*

*Ps 69:1

*Cf. Bernard, Asspt 14; OB 5:273.

*Is 53:4

*Sg 5:10

*Is 53:12

3. Yet something much more humiliating lies hidden within this shame. For by the will of God the Father thus providing for us something better than our utmost hope could have envisaged, all the sins of all of us were bound tightly together, and he bowed his neck beneath them. Go forth, daughters of Sion,* and behold something strange, a great marvel that must strike with utter amazement all who see it, angels as well as men. God the Father has sat down upon the judgment seat on his high and exalted throne. He has summoned Jesus, who stands in readiness before his Father. Around him press the whole heavenly army, eager to hear what new thing that day is to be achieved or decreed.

*Sg 3:11

The Father speaks to his Son: 'The cry of the sons of Israel,* o my Son, has thundered in my ears, it has moved my heart with its bitter misery. I will no longer let my anger restrain my mercy, because this is the time well-pleasing to me in which I send you, my only son, into the world. My son, I am sending you to your brothers, my sons, who have gone down into the pit,* and there await you, my promised one. But for the sake of those who will have to descend thither unless you go before them, it is this day necessary for you to become like those who go into the pit. Furthermore, the iniquity of the daughter of Sion* is so exceedingly great in my sight that there is no way in which it can be expiated except in your self abasement, in your blood. It is for this that I am sending you, my one spotless lamb, that in you I may reconcile to myself whomever I have destined for salvation.'

*Ex 3:9

*Cf. Ps 30:3

*Cf. Lm 4:22

Then he who sat upon the throne gave orders that the huge sack containing all the sins of Adam and his sons, which had been sealed and hidden in the royal treasury, should be brought out into their midst. He ordered then that planks also should be brought, and the sword. When all this had been done, the king said to his Son: 'You see before you the sack of your race, sealed. Unseal it, take out all that is in it, examine it, count it, weigh it. As I live, I shall require all these things from you, and you will bear all this iniquity. Therefore pierce your hand and wound your foot;

groan, blush for shame, and do penance for all of this. You are my firstborn, my only Son, and I have given all things into your hands. But in this exchange I shall not spare or pity you. I shall take into account nothing but your appearance. Behold, accept these planks for your cross, inasmuch as your father transgressed through a tree, and under a tree your mother was corrupted.* Finally, I have unsheathed this sword once and for ever, that it may drink deep of your blood. As far as I am concerned, all this is fixed and immutable; "What I have written, I have written." '*

*Cf. Gn 3:6*

*Jn 19:22*

4. At this pronouncement of the king, so dread and inflexible against his only Son, the whole court of heaven stood aghast and trembled. But he, standing with deep attention by the judgment seat, immediately prostrated himself on the ground in adoration, bending his knees before his Father and stretching out his hands. 'Everything,' he said, 'concerning me, everything in me, be done according to your will, o my Father. For as you know, Lord, "my meat is to do your will".* For this I have come, for this I live. And first of all, this sack of sin which you have placed upon me, although large and heavy, I take up with glad devotion. I will do penance for these sins in your sight, enduring most patiently, even entreating most earnestly, that everything be laid at my door as much as at the door of my father and brothers.

*Jn 4:34*

'At your command, I have [opened the

sack] examined everything in it, gazed at
the terrible appearance of those sins,
counted their number one by one, weighed
their bulk: In your presence I grieve over
them and am exceedingly confounded, but
in you, o Lord my Father, I have hoped,
knowing I shall not be confounded for
ever.* It is right and just that all the    *Ps 30:2*
judgment you have passed up till now on
Adam and his sons has been wholly one of
confusion and loss. But now, Lord, protect the presence of your Son from the
foul and dreadful presence of my sins, for
your mercy is powerful and lovely in its
purifying action. Even if my sins are more
numerous than the hairs of my head,*    *Cf. Ps 40:12*
your mercies are more numerous still by
far, making my head rise above them. Even
if the burden of them is overwhelmingly
heavy and difficult to bear, greater without comparison, Father, is your mercy, so
that I may win pardon in your eyes. As for
the planks and the sword, which you have
prepared and offered to your Son, My
heart is ready, o God, my heart is ready.*    *Ps 108:1*
There is only one favor I crave of your
goodness: grant that your wrath may pass
over to me, and be diverted from your
people. In my blood may all your creatures
be reconciled to you in peace, so that
my blood be the sign and everlasting cause
of the eternal covenant between us.'*    *Cf. Heb 9:14*

5. He finished speaking, and all who
heard were lost in wonder at the willing
obedience of such great majesty. The angels
in the judgment hall reeled in their seats,

and they began to say to one another:
'Truly this is the Son of God,* for his very
speech betrays him.'* But the Father,
recollecting in his heart all the words and
feelings and compliances of his Son, was
stirred in the depths of his being. Indeed,
his heart yearned for his son,* and he cried
aloud: 'By myself I swear it, because you
have done this* and not spared your soul
because of me nor obeyed flesh and blood
rather than my voice, in your deed all the
earth will be blessed. Though by this
exchange you will eat your bread in the
sweat of your brow,* yet to this sweat of
yours the earth will soon respond and from
this day its fruit will be spontaneous and
everlasting. Consequently, because of you,
I forgive men all my anger, and I will no
longer hold in memory the old complaint.
But it is not enough for me that you bring
back to life the tribes of Jacob, but rather
that in you and your obedience, the whole
family of the earth should be blessed. But
this is not enough in my eyes, because it is
my good pleasure to restore all things in
heaven by your blood and to bring peace
to things in heaven and things on earth.*
From this day forth I myself will judge no
one, but I give all judgment to you. I give
you a name so glorious as to be above
every name, which every tongue will confess, before which every knee will bow.*

After these words there was great exultation, joy and rejoicing in heaven, such as
has not been from the beginning of creation, rejoicing first over the ineffable

*Mk 15:39
*Mt 26:73

*1 Kg 3:26

*Gn 22:16

*Gn 3:19

*Cf. Ep 1:20

*Cf. Ph 2:9-11

goodness of the Father, then over the wonderful obedience of the Son, thirdly over the reconciliation of human nature, fourthly over the restoration of the celestial city. So the sound of the wings of the cherubim was heard from afar, and the whole city was stirred with the cries of exultation, with the shouts of praise and thanksgiving.

6. Meanwhile my spirit burnt within me to seek out and discover, if this was at all possible, what was the reason for this overwhelming and mysterious sentence that the Father passed on his Son. For what was the logic of a law or the quality of a sentence by which, though I am the one guilty of death, another is given up to death on my behalf? With full knowledge and deliberation I have committed murder: how is it that I am released, and the blood that I have shed is demanded of another? I have stolen from my Lord a very large sum of money, ten thousand talents. I am caught with the evidence of my theft and dragged to the court. I am patently guilty, everyone pronounces sentence on me. The cross is prepared, I am immediately hauled to it with my hands bound. I am pale at the nearness of death and no idea but that of death is present to my eyes. Lo and behold, suddenly a voice rings out from the throne, ordering me to be brought back and released, while someone else, who has done nothing wrong, is dragged to the gibbet and fastened to the cross. Where is the appearance of justice here, what manner of

judgment is this?

We read also in scripture, where the prophet speaks in the person of the Lord God: 'The soul that sins shall die, the righteousness of the righteous shall be upon himself, and the wickedness of the wicked shall be upon himself.'* But here the order is reversed, with the righteousness of the righteous falling upon the wicked and the wickedness of the wicked upon the righteous. There is the case, too, of Abraham, that friend of God most high, who spoke with him as a man speaks with his friend. He put it to God that the just should not perish with the wicked and he added: 'This is not your way, you who judge all the earth.'* Does it not seem equally inconsistent that the just should perish for the wicked as that he should perish with him? The fathers have eaten sour grapes, and the teeth of the children are set on edge*— surely that ancient proverb, which the Lord swore to make void in Israel, has not been given a fresh lease on life by the very one who emptied it of meaning? For all of us have eaten sour grapes, and it is innocent teeth, teeth whiter than milk, that are set on edge.

7. I am speaking to you, o Lord my God, although I am but dust and ashes. I beseech you, hear me patiently. If justice and right are the foundation of your throne,* and sitting on the throne of justice you absolve the guilty and condemn the innocent, then show me, o most holy, with what justice you have done it. I see indeed

*Ezk 18:4;20

*Cf. Hos 1:4

*Ezk 18:2

*Ps 89:14

that in all this I have been treated very mercifully, but as you show mercy, show also the reason for the mercy, show its justice. I believe that in heaven, in your own domain, you have some new kind of justice, not revealed before that time but to be revealed on the day of salvation with salvation itself. For so we read of your promise in scripture: 'Soon my salvation will come and my justice will be revealed.'* *Is 56:1 And again: 'The Lord has made known his salvation; in the sight of all the peoples he has revealed his justice.'* And at this I *Ps 97:2 seem to hear the voice of the Lord answering me in my inner ear and saying to me: 'O man, my charity, this is my justice. From the beginning I so loved the world* *Cf. Jn 3:16 as to give my only Son, first to mortality, then to death, even the death of the cross.* *Ph 2:8 Him alone I have found a man after my own heart,* a just man to all generations, *Ac 13:22 distinguished among thousands, whether of men or angels, one both able and willing to fulfil my will and become my salvation in heaven and on earth. Or is it not lawful to me to do what I please?* Who would *Mt 20:15 wish to set a limit to my kindness and love, to lay down a law?'

I give you thanks, Lord God, for this most gracious reply, and for the incomprehensible depths of your mercy. I see, I clearly see, that your charity is your justice, since indeed you are all charity, our God, you are all justice. With you to abound with the riches of mercy is absolutely just, because proper, natural and instinctive. Thus it was in the truest sense your justice to hand over your only Son as a ransom for us all, and it was the justice of that only Son of yours freely to obey his Father's will so lovingly and effectively. At your command he pursued even unto death the iniquity of mankind, so hateful to your holiness; he affixed it with him to the cross, and utterly removed it from your sight by his blood. This is why we too sing to our spouse, your Son, crying out with great joy: 'You have loved justice and hated wickedness, therefore God, your God, has anointed you with the oil of gladness above your fellows.'* Therefore, as was just, you have given him the first fruits of universal joy, immediately transforming his flesh with the oil of your anointing, establishing him as the first-born from the dead,* the cause and beginning of all who will share with him in rising from the dead to incorruption. He is thus your beloved, and the beloved of your holy church, and the beloved of every holy soul, radiant from his immaculate conception, red from his voluntary passion, glowing and flaming with the love of your justice, namely, the obedience of his will. Passionate in his hatred of sin—that is, in expiating it, ardently burning in the joy of the resurrection, he is above all his fellows. May we become partakers with him, we beg you, most holy Father, beseeching it through the charity of your only Son, who with you lives and reigns, in the unity of the Holy Spirit, God for ever and ever. Amen.

*Ps 45:7

*Col 1:18

## SERMON ELEVEN

*The beginning of the eleventh sermon.* Of the inestimable worth of charity, of its brightness, weight and strength. That gold, or, in other words, charity, should be offered to God alone, for he alone is lovable. Of the different reasons for loving God.

'HIS HEAD is the finest gold.* When the bride is questioned by the daughters of Jerusalem about the grace and beauty of her beloved, she addresses herself to his praise with all her strength, especially because nothing is sweeter than to be totally free to behold what he is like, and to reply to those who have the same holy leisure. So at the head of her praise, she thinks it best to begin from the head. (Certainly what she first said about her beloved being radiant and ruddy was by way of prologue, a sort of indication that there was much still to be said.) 'His head is the finest gold,'* she therefore says. But how meagerly she chooses to describe such great majesty, particularly of that member which is the particular seat of beauty, the focal-point of strength and dignity. Is it not to be feared that this introduction will cause the daughters of Jerusalem to feel surprised

*Sg 5:11

*Sg 5:11

displeasure rather than edification or admiration? May they not justifiably complain in private: 'All very well for idols, but how does it interest us? Why do you thrust gold upon us now, as if we were to fashion in our hearts a golden image of your beloved? Let the king of Babylon and his courtiers have a dream of a golden head and its interpretation,* but for us who are yearning for the revelation of the face of the spouse, do not produce entangling delays or this kind of comparison. If you will permit us to be quite frank, o fairest among women, when you become intoxicated and lost in God, do you not also forget to speak as well as to think of us in our neediness and longing? You have certainly been taken into the wine cellars of your spouse; let the heady draught with which you are soaked subside a little, and be soberly mindful of your daughters, hanging on your words.'

*Cf. Dn 2

But the bride has an immediate rejoinder ready: 'I am speaking to you with the voice of my spouse. Are you still without intelligence? So long a time have I been with you* and will you not yet allow yourselves to be weaned? Certainly, as long as you remembered the breast and its milk, you could not take more solid food. Now, I see well, your time has come, the time of lovers,* when you have matured and learned to sigh now for your spouse and ask so eagerly about his beauty. Here certainly is the Spirit, strongly drawing you to these things, this, indeed, is the

*Mt 15:16

*Cf. Ezk 16:8

spirit of wisdom. You have also received the spirit of understanding, even though you are concealing it, or are rather slack in acting upon it.'

Come then, brothers, let us too, as far as we may, be numbered among these maidens on fire with holy love. Let us too, according to the bride's words, follow the spirit of understanding, in conformity to the principles of faith. Let us follow it as a star from heaven, until we enter the sanctuary of God,* and can find and adore this truth, concealed beneath a sacred veil, as if it were Jesus, wrapped in swaddling clothes.* There is no doubt that if our hand can find that gold of which the bride speaks, my king will be most gracious in his recompense.

2. Not to keep you in suspense any longer, there is nothing I take in more easily from the bride than that gold should be used by us to designate charity. Certainly, manifold grounds lead me to this conclusion. Charity, just like gold, is precious, is full of light, is weighty, is solid, and once purged by fire, has learned to resist it.

Indeed, if we are to consider its value, as long as it has found a merchant who is careful, wise, rich and daring, it is more precious than all the wealth there is. Nothing we can desire is fit to be compared with it. But how can I probe into its price, since no man knows the price of it*, certainly not he who is of the earth and has only learned to speak of earthly things.*

*Cf. Ps 73:16*

*Lk 2:12*

*Jb 23:13*

*Cf. Jb 3:31*

Let the question be put rather to him who
has crossed the sea, triumphing over our
death by his own. He set its value above
that of choice gold, for when he sat down
at his Father's right hand, it was charity he
diffused into the hearts of his elect. For
this is truly that pearl of great price, which
is deservedly obtained by selling everything. That excellent merchant, the only
one to value his goods aright, considered
that this one good was to be preferred to all
the rest. From so great a recommendation
by so great a merchant, the repute of its
value has drawn after him an infinite crowd
of merchants who, having sold all, bear
in their hand the price of the pearl, namely,
contempt of the world, leading even to
contempt of themselves, and in this way,
they lay hold of it.* If among them is
found one who says: 'It is worthless, it is
worthless'—as the custom always is for a
buyer—'It is worthless, it is expensive, it is
a hard bargain' yet once he has taken the
pearl from the hand of the merchant, he
immediately changes his tune and says: 'It
is fine, it is inexpensive, it is a delightful
bargain'. Whoever makes a deal with me is
always the loser. "What I sell is valueless,
yet I have purchased goods of inestimable
value."† For if a man should give all the
substance of his house for love, he would
account it as nothing.*

3.  Charity then is full of light, in that it
effortlessly shows up the darkness of sin,
reveals the paths of justice in the beams of
its brightness, and makes the loving soul

vividly aware of eternal life by a certain inner vision of it. We have the testimony of John, that 'whoever loves his brother sees God.'* How much more does he who loves God, see God! At the same time, observe that the light of gold is neither fed from one source or diminished from another, but has within itself an everlasting source and a power of shining with a glorious natural splendor. Externally it shines out to others, but nonetheless internally it shines for itself. In these qualities, is not the image of light-giving charity mirrored with great brightness? For charity, radiant in the witness of her own conscience, neither rests on the praise of others nor loses any of her peculiar glory through their censure. Although that which shows on the outside is bright, much brighter still is that which lies within, certainly keeping some little light for the world without, but retaining a great deal for its own inner illumination.

*Jn 4:20

Then, too, charity is heavy, with a weight that bears it up to things of eternity. For, as a wise man has said:* there is a weight upwards just as there is a weight downwards. Fire and water are both moved by their weights, one straining to things above, the other whirling swiftly down to things below. Hence for a thinking being its love is its weight. The current of his love carries each one away, and as a pagan says: 'His own desire is what draws a man.'* Blessed indeed is charity, which draws us to Christ, and draws and pulls with more efficacious power the more it calls upon

*Augustine, Confessions 13,9; PL 32: 848-9.

*Virgil, Eclogue 2, l. 65.

the hand of him by whom it is drawn, to whom it draws, saying: 'Draw me after you.'* So charity is extremely weighty, since by the force of its own spirit it frees itself from things of earth for those of heaven. Not even there does it take its stand, but hastens on to him who sits at the Father's right hand through the tireless momentum of its weight, and in him finally rests. Here it can say: 'From this place I remember that I came forth, joyfully do I flow back again. This is the place of my birth, this is the goal of my endeavor, this is the resting place of my abode. Beneath this nothing pleases, and outside this nothing delights; beyond this nothing is agreeable, within this is whatever most deeply and richly satisfies.'

4. Next, charity is solid. It may be fretted by annoyance, but it simply cannot be worn away. Like gold, if you batter at it, you broaden it; if you strike at it, you do not cut it but lengthen it. If you persist in striking, it also persists in increasing. In a wonderful way, it turns all its losses into abundant profit, whether beaten with hammers or thrust into the fire. Indeed, when it is beaten, its substance expands just as gold does, and the splendor lying hid within bursts forth into view. So through suffering and endurance, charity grows in a double fashion; it grows, let me repeat, in charity, and grows also in clarity. Again, after various hammer-blows of trouble, if the fire of fiercer tribulation seize it, it knows that this is to test it, not to consume

*Sg 1:3

it. Fire can only devour what is weak and base, but here it has no power at all, being given over to serve, to purify, to burnish. But when all impurities have been refined away by heat, fire is of no use to it, and of no harm, either. There is no further service it can render save that which tends to glory, to the completeness of victory, to a marvellous triumph. Whoever now draws near will be able to see, with Moses, a great and awesome sight: how charity, like gold, burns and is not consumed.* For it reigns uncurbed, and from this day forth only triumphs over fire and says: 'More than that, we rejoice in our tribulations'.* And so, finally, persuaded by these arguments, I agree that the gold the bride speaks of is charity.

*Cf. Ex 3:3

*Rm 5:3

5. Yet there is another argument, no less forceful, which affects me no less forcefully, whether rightly or not you can yourselves decide. I have heard, and made a mental note of it, that when the bride was still very young, and her breasts were first beginning to swell, she was then only entering upon that state of love which is now hers. She did not yet speak familiarly to her spouse, and her condition was only one of desire, not yet of fruition. In her interior soliloquies, she kept her mind active, constantly repeating, with great fear: 'Let him kiss me with the kiss of his mouth.'* I have heard, too, that in those days the bride betook herself to Bezalel,† so that from a little gold which she had, he might make golden ear-rings for her. Her

*Sg 1:1
†Cf. Ex 36

intention was to win the favor of her beloved, so that when he saw her so adorned, the king would desire her beauty.*

*Ps 45:10*

And then she turned her mind to golden necklaces and bracelets and rings, to a dress of cloth of gold, with golden fringes*

*Cf. Ps 45:14*

and all the other trappings of an elegant woman that could wound the heart of the beloved.*

*Cf. Sg 4:9*

But since at that time she was still young and poor, she did in the meantime what she could. Hence, when the wicked spun their stories, and the empty-minded their scurrilities, and the evil tried to hiss into her ear the malignant mutter of their whisperings, she straightway laid firm hold on the golden souvenirs of her beloved, which dangle, as it were, in the ears of her heart. She used to say: 'This gate shall remain shut.'* And only my beloved, when he comes, shall enter through it, or some-

*Ezk 44:2*

one who comes from his side, speaking of his kingdom. Such a man—if he speaks of his justice or his strength, his humility or goodness, and especially if he begins to speak of his love and the good treasure of his heart brings forth the goodly theme of my beloved's charity for me—may cer-

*Cf. Mt 12:35*

tainly enter.*

Her hope is not disappointed. When the Lord sees her thus attired, and so carefully following him and seeking his face, he thinks her worthy of the kiss of his mouth for which she has longed, and she becomes united and made one with him. In a word, as we have heard and do believe, she has entered into the joy of her Lord\*, she has been made free of all the possessions of her beloved, and she overflows with all delight. Blissfully she enjoys her spouse, judging herself to know but him alone, and clinging to him with whom she is become one spirit.\*

Hearing this and very many similar things, I must confess I have been on fire with desire for the reward of this gold. Why should anyone, even the poorest of the poor, not venture at least to desire it? Although I am wretched and pitiable and poor and blind and naked and overcome with shame, not enduring the disgrace of my poverty, I have gone right up to the good counsellor. Weeping before him, I have exposed my utter destitution, and heard from him his word of good counsel. 'My advice', he says, 'is to buy from me gold tried in the fire, that you may be rich.'\* And he added: 'If you sell all the substance of your house,\* what you desire will be done.' Accordingly I went away and set my hand resolutely to the work.\* I could not as yet sell everything, as I hoped, because my furnishings were various and difficult to remove from my house, but I am continually busy about them. I keep at it, if somehow in the end I may grasp something of the prize.\* You, too, brothers, are very well acquainted with that excellent counsellor and merchant, for he has assuredly said the same to you and, unless I am wrong, the same rivalry for that enkindled gold of his drives you on. He is a

*\*Mt 25:21*

*\*Cf. 1 Co 6:17*

*\*Rv 3:18*
*\*Cf. Sg 8:7*

*\*Pr 31:19*

*\*Cf. Ph 3:14*

great king, the richest of all kings, who has such a store, such an infinite treasure of gold, that in his sight silver is accounted worthless.* If one should speak with the tongues of angels, but have not charity,* in his sight such a man is as though he did not exist.*

*Cf. Ws 7:9
*1 Co 13:1

*Cf. Is 40:17

In the land where he lives, there is gold, and the gold of that country is very good.* But when he came down to our level and deigned to become a little child in our midst, without delay an edict came from his Father in heaven that all the gold that was anywhere on the earth was to be brought at once to the son of the king and placed in his treasury. This was clearly very just and beneficial. To him alone all love is rightly due. By him alone it was created, and created for this sole purpose, and then only is it blessed when totally poured out for him alone. Deservedly, then, ought it to be considered theft if someone does not bring all his gold to the king, but hides it away secretly to make an idol of it.* Anyone, therefore, who heard the sound of this edict thundered from heaven, did not spare his treasures, but with eager rivalry they came from the corners of the earth to lay their treasures before the king. They came from the east and from the north, some from Arabia, others from Saba, many from Tharsis.*

*Gn 2:11-12

*Cf. Ho 2:8

*Cf. Ps 72:10

6. Since love is the natural property of the king alone, and he alone is wholly to be desired, everything in heaven and on earth offers an incentive to love for those who

long to love him. Each one takes to himself, in different ways, the spur of loving,
according as he receives it from heaven.
Some from the very beginning have come
running to offer him their love, still in its
first freshness, and from that in itself they
derive an incentive to love, knowing that
they could not have loved him in this way
had they not first been loved by him and
set apart. So those who came from the
east are the first-fruits of his lovers. They
hastened when Jesus was still a baby to
consecrate to him the first dawn of their
beginning, and grasping at once that he too
was beginning, they followed him where-
soever he goes.* This, then, is the gold      *Rv 14:4*
which the wise men from the east offered
to the king of heaven in his manger.*        *Cf. Mt 2:11*

'From the north', also, as Job tells us,
'comes gold,'* but those who bear it,         *Jb 37:22*
coming from a land so far away, cannot
arrive so quickly. Still, the later they begin
their journey, the more swiftly they travel,
and the more fervently they run. From
this they draw very great matter for loving,
as they would not have been summoned
from such a great distance had they not
been intimately known and loved. Nor can
the thought of such love ever leave their
memory, for he who has taken pity on
them has said: 'to the north, "Give up",
and to the south, "Do not hold back." '*     *Is 43:6*
Indeed, the south does ill to hold back, and
holding back will not be heard, if my Lord,
according to the riches of his bounty,
should wish to give to me just as also to

him. My brother does ill to be moved against my Father, if he bestows on me also the grace which of his bounty he has kept for him. But in this case it happens that my brother thinks he does well to be moved, because my Father offers me greater reason to love. He fears for himself, thinking that since I come from distant lands with a richer supply of gold, my greater love will make me loved more; or, to put it more truly, because I am loved more, I will have a greater love. To confess the truth, I have no doubt that I am bound to a greater love. In short, I know that as far as I am concerned, this is the one thing necessary.* I beg most merciful Father night and day, and shall not cease to beg, that he who gave the motive, will also give the reality.

But there is one point I think I should observe more carefully He who from the east came to Jesus arising from his mother, hastened and ran before me to take possession of the sight of Jesus lying in the manger or sucking at his mother's breast. In the same way, my particular possession is his death and burial and resurrection, with the thief and Mary Magdalen at the cross of Christ. Here is where I shall find healing for my wounds, forgiveness for my sins, an end to my old life, the hope of a new beginning.

7. What is to be said about 'the gold of Arabia'?* Why does it say: 'It will be given to him *from* the gold of Arabia', and not just 'gold of Arabia'? I think it is because a

*Lk 10:42

*Ps 72:15

small quantity was brought to him from there, and he who spoke in this way through the Holy Spirit has indicated this. For what is that 'Arabia', which gave so little—though choice quality—gold to our king? Might it be she of whom the apostle speaks: 'Sinai is a mountain in Arabia', associated with that Jerusalem which is in bondage with her children?* It fits very well, as she has given our king a little gold from her store, but that little is of the best and very pure. For Isaiah said: 'There is a holy seed which remains in her,* a seed which the Lord has blessed,'* and in which the Lord has blessed all her kindred throughout the earth. As far as this gold is concerned, he gave it abundantly in his own regard who said: 'Who shall separate us from the love of Christ?'* Opening up his great stores of gold, he revealed many things and discussed their depths, and he found no end to his treasures. But that huge crowd, which stood with Jesus in the level ground*, meaning Arabia, could not go up to him on the mountain and understand the heights of perfection. They were not strong enough to give all their gold to our king, but they gave him from their gold the trifling amount they could manage. He, most generous in giving, is likewise most gracious in accepting. He rejects no offering, however small, as long as it is from their gold.* Fittingly this verse continues: 'They shall pray for him without ceasing.'* Since they cannot worship him on his holy mountain,* they will in the meantime

*Ga 4:25

*Is 6:13
*Is 61:9

*Rm 8:35

*Lk 6:17

*Cf. Ps 72:15
*Ps 72:15

*Ps 99:9

*Ps 99:5*

worship at his footstool, for that is holy.*

8. I have yet to treat of the gold coming from Saba and from Tharsis, but the length of my sermon, the lateness of the hour and consideration for you, my hearers, hold me back. So the conclusion of this sermon will be the introduction to the one that follows. You must pray to the only Son of the Father that he may grant us something worthy of himself which we can share with you for our salvation and to his glory, who with the Father and the Holy Spirit lives in joyful glory, God, for ever and ever.
Amen.

## SERMON TWELVE

*The beginning of the twelfth sermon.* What
manifold proof there is that gold in this context signifies charity. Why all from Saba are
said to be rich in gold. What are the ships of
Tharsis and how difficult it is to sail them.
How powerful charity is in heaven, how
weak among us, so that there 'his head is of
the finest gold,'* but here 'his feet are        *Sg 5:11*
like burnished bronze.'*                         *Rv 1:15*

'HIS HEAD is of finest gold.'*         *Sg 5:11*
Inevitably, the prayers of lovers,
or of those who desire to love,
give a glad welcome to whatever serves to
expound love, provided it does not go
beyond the boundaries of faith and the
safe path of scripture. I have no regrets at
having identified gold as charity when I
consider whose term it was, of whom she
used it, what its substance was, and,
finally, to whom she spoke. Without doubt
it was a loved woman who spoke, she spoke
about her beloved, she spoke to those living for love, or at least longing for it.
What wonder if she identifies love as
gold, especially when speaking of the head
of her beloved? For what is more lovable
than love, what is dearer than charity, what
is sweeter, stronger, more light-giving? You

215

will remember that I discussed some of these points with you in the preceding sermon. That sermon ended with a promise that, after the gold coming from the east and from the north and from Arabia, something would in turn be said, for your love, about what was brought to Christ the king from Saba and from Tharsis.

My first point is this: above all the lands mentioned so far, the land of Saba is blessed in this, that not a few came from her with gold, not even many, but all. For thus it is written: 'All from Saba shall come, bearing gold and incense.'* What land do you take this to be if not that where, as report declares and scripture witnesses, incense customarily springs? What is the land of incense if not devotion in praying, frequency in praying, purity of prayer and earnestness in prayer? Already your charity has noticed, I would imagine, that it is not surprising that gold should abound in a place where it can be purchased simply and solely by a trade in incense. It is not a matter here of a little from the handful of incense which is laid in the thurible, but with both hands there is thrown into the furnace a generous, full amount from the hill of incense, so that prayer may be directed as incense before God, and the lifting up of the hands as an evening sacrifice.* I put it to you, why should charity not abound in someone to whom it has already been granted to desire it more than anything else that pleases? He seeks it from one who is rich in charity, he persistently begs it from one who has

*Is 60:6

*Ps 141:2

himself commanded it, he wrests it vio-
lently from one who has directed that force
should be used against himself. I think
this is enough to make it clear why all the
inhabitants of this region are both so
wealthy that they have a rich supply of
gold and so faithful and loyal to our king
that they come running humbly to offer
him the gold with which their country
abounds.

But if gold is purchased with incense,
why is what buys gold not placed before
it? Why does it say: 'gold and incense', and
not rather: 'incense and gold'? For this
reason—unless I am mistaken—that the
purity of prayer and the sweetness of love
earnestly seek mutual support and make a
reciprocal agreement as to what each is
worth. Before pure prayer can be uttered, it
must of necessity be forestalled by the
spirit of charity, for this it is that utters
it, that sets the incense burning, that directs
its smoke. Likewise, before charity can be
a living flame, sweet-scented and worthy of
the heavenly altars, there must of necessity
be the incense of prayer. You may well ask
what could be more pleasant, effective or
profitable than this buying and selling? By
the urgency of your prayer, you are laying
up for yourself a rich treasure of charity,
and the more abundant the charity, the
more frequent the prayer, the more powerful its effect, the more perfect its purity,
the more delightful its sweetness.

2. From this country came that woman
whom the gospel praises: 'her price is from

*Pr 31:10*

the far off coasts',* since, as scripture tells us: 'she came from the ends of the earth to

*Mt 12:42*

hear the wisdom of Solomon.'* Therefore our Solomon, Christ, found her a noble woman, for she made ready for the first Solomon. Why was it, do you think, that she longed so much to see the face of Solomon and hear the grace poured out

*Ps 44:2*

upon his lips;* and then, when she had the privilege of seeing and hearing him, why did she feel that there was no more spirit

*Cf. 1 K 10:5*

in her*? It was because she inhabited the land of Saba, the country of incense. And she was not just an inhabitant either, but a queen. Hence it also follows that she came to Solomon laden with spices, more precious than had before her time been borne

*Cf. 1 K 10:10*

to Jerusalem.* She offered them to the king, and carried home with her far richer gifts from him.

Here we can see the quality of prayer, its greatness and power. How sweet a fragrance this incense has! It makes us long to behold the king of Jerusalem, and then it grants us what we long for. As we come it loads us with precious spices; as we go it loads us with joys more precious still. I am ashamed, brothers, of our poverty in this matter. We appear to be holding in our hands instrumetns of sacred song and lyres of prayer, but to our shame we have hung up our lyres on the willow trees of vain

*Cf. Ps 137:2*

thoughts and affections.* Our enemies laugh in our face and lead us around captive wherever they please. If their scorn leaves us unmoved, why are we not at least affected by the presence of the friends who listen to us, and by respect for the holy angels who hear and join us in praise? It is a shameful thing to have to say, but in the middle of our chant our harp falls silent. We seem indeed to be keeping vigil: there is resounding plainsong on our lips, but in our hearts it sleeps. Awake, my glory, awake, lyre and harp,* how long until you are awake? If I wanted to glory in you, and knew how to do it, surely you would be my glory now, and my hope of glory in the world to come. Meanwhile, all this about the power of prayer has been by way of digression in the sermon, because speaking of the gold of Saba led also to a mention of incense.

*Ps 108:2

3. If gold from Saba is so precious, what are we to think of the gold from Tharsis? Gold is native there, and it was from there that Solomon brought huge quantities of gold to Jerusalem in his ships.* For this ships were certainly necessary, but these were built by Solomon himself by his wisdom and steered across the sea by his prudence. Can we regard these ships as anything other than frequent, earnest meditations, directed towards increasing the treasures of charity? With Solomon arranging all the business, they were sent to Tharsis—that is to say, the country of joy, according to the meaning of the name, 'Tharsis'—so that they might zealously seek for joy throughout the whole land. This country of joy is surely no other than that which was spoken of

*Cf. 1 K 10:22

to Israel: 'Learn where there is wisdom and where there is prudence, so that at the same time you may discern where there is length of days, and life, where there is light for the eyes and peace'?* This is truly the country of joy, or rather, this country is joy, for so we rejoice to read of her: 'For behold,' says the Lord, 'I create Jerusalem a rejoicing, and her people a joy.'*

And so the ships of Solomon were sent thither, under the fair wind of the spirit of charity, to search out the gold which is native there, to buy it, and to bring it by sea to Jerusalem, with Solomon in command of the voyage both ways. Otherwise these ships would have been in great danger. As they came and went across a vast sea, endless in its infinity of thoughts and desires, salty with deep bitterness, swollen with excitement, choppy with uncertainties, temptestuous with disorders, they would have had to fear lest with a strong wind the Lord should overturn the ships of Tharsis.* And indeed it is a strong wind of the spirit that says: 'In the power of my hand I have done it, and in my wisdom I have understood.'* Of this spirit Isaiah says the same: 'The spirit of the strong is like a storm beating down a wall.'*

4. O dust and ashes, with all your pride! How long will you keep rushing into a man and undermining your own self? Your wall is tumbling down through what you have done yourself, and dangerously tilted through the evil spirit. How

*Ba 3:14

*Is 65:18

*Ps 48:7

*Is 10:13

*Is 25:4

long will you keep making it worse, throwing your weight against it to beat it down
and overthrow it? Against this powerful
spirit it is essential to have the spirit of
truth and gentleness, always secretly calling
upon grace while crossing the sea, still
invoking grace while engaged on the search,
again and again offering thanks for the
grace of God while coming home. Thus in
every place, as Solomon says: 'the man of
discernment will control the helm',* and          *Pr 1:5
the spirit of Jesus, a spirit all gentle and
humble, will command the wind and the
sea, and there will be a great calm, every-
thing will be safe.* If grace were not in          *Cf. Mt 8:24-26
command, always supporting you, there
would be danger for your soul and for
everything in the ship, in embarking on this
voyage, exposing yourself to winds and so
vast a sea. But if you have wisdom, Jesus
will go before you in the ship, and taking
his seat as an oarsman, will hold the
rudder. But do not let him sleep or grow
drowsy there, in case while he slumbers a
storm arises, the waves rush in and the
tempest overwhelms you.* How many and          *Cf. Mt 8:24-26
how great are the evils which this powerful
wind causes to those who sail to Tharsis
and to those who return from Tharsis to
Jerusalem with rich treasure! What great
things we have heard and known;* we          *Ps 78:3
remember them and tremble.

Take for example Solomon himself, who
from the infinite treasures of wisdom and
knowledge bestowed on him by God composed this nuptial hymn. A powerful wind

of the spirit suddenly overtook him in a
ship heavy-laden with gold, and suddenly
he was wrecked. Unless he had been taken
into the treasure-house of charity, how
could he really have sung aloud to us such
beautiful and noble things about charity?
Almost every word of them, whether in a
heart that loves or on lips that speak or in
the hand that writes them, is like a rich
vein of gold. How did it happen, that in the
very first man to handle this gold, the gold
has become dim, its pure color has faded?*
Now I am not arguing as to whether he is
saved or lost, but I do most heartily wish
that his salvation was as certain as the certainty of his overthrow. But, my brothers,
I pray that his ruin and that of those like
him, may be a support to us. Even to this
day he kindles us to love by his glowing
eloquence; may he teach us by his terrible
downfall the fear of the Lord.

    However, we must not so completely
give way to fear as not to apply ourselves
also in every possible way to love, but
on the contrary. This undertaking is all the
more to be desired in that it must be
carried out with zeal and discretion. Consequently, as long as I hear eternal happiness offered to me on a condition, and it is
said to me: 'Do this and this, and you will
live;' as long as I hear that I can have no
certainty about the future and I am warned
not to count on tomorrow, so long do I not
rely upon my life. Rather, my soul chooses
to hang,* and day and night my life will be
hanging in doubt before my eyes.* Even if

*Lm 4:1

*Jb 7:15
*Cf. Dt 28:66

the Lord opened for me the flood-gates of heaven, and freely poured down on me as much rain as I could desire, if he gave proofs of his goodwill towards me, increasing them, blessing my soul,* I remain unaltered in my conviction that the more he blesses me, the more I should be fearful. In proportion as the Lord breathes on me, and the spirit of this fear begins to blow through me and to fill and possess my senses, I will more safely and boldly open my mouth wide.* Since this gift comes from heaven, I will open as wide as I can, in order to draw the spirit of love in the desire of my soul.

So, brothers, if at any time the ships of Tharsis come to grief, let us not on that account drop the whole undertaking or engage in it with less enthusiasm. Many women have gathered together riches,* but that woman who is compared to the ship of a merchant*, she has outdone them all.† Yes, the harbor to which meditations happily steer is nothing else than the investigation of joy. The goal of this blissful meditation is nothing else than the fruit of holy contemplation, which is charity, and you know the sons of charity. Their names are joy, peace, patience, tolerance, kindness, integrity, and many like them, whom the apostle enumerates.*

5. But in this investigation of joy, the question arises, and must be answered, as to what should be investigated more carefully, or rather, which gold outweighs which, which gold outshines which, which

*Cf. Ml 3:10

*Cf. Ps 85:17

*Pr 31:29

*Pr 31:14
†Pr 31:29

*Gl 5:22

gold stands out for purity. In that country
of eternal joy, in which all find their
home, rejoicing,* surely the gold which is
found there is the best.* There, nothing
can be added to its purity, particularly
since there is nowhere there where gold
can be manufactured. Hence it is that in
the temple of the true Solomon, which is
constructed of plated gold, everything is of
gold most pure. 'The cherubim overshadowing the mercy-seat,' and the ark of the
covenant, and the golden candlestick, and
all the vessels of the temple,* all are of
purest gold, because they are of purest
charity. For charity reigns as queen over
everything in that country; she pours herself over all, and translates the whole into
herself, so that charity may be all in all.*

6. O Lord, my God, you know how,
with the deepest love, poor though that
love be, I have loved from my inmost heart
the beauty of your house.* I love it still,
and my soul longs and pines for your
courts.* But I myself know and confess
from the heart that that beauty is something to be hungered after; anything I
attempt in loving it is very little. Yet you
are the Father of lights, from whom is this
best gift.* At the time and in the manner
you please, you will increase it in me as
is possible, even if it is still very slight
according to the measure of your giving
and my own capacity.* Then I will love
your house with a mighty love, I will
deserve to drink deep drafts of it and to
feast on the beginnings of your glory.*

*Ps 87:7
*Cf. Gn 2:12

*Heb 9:5

*Cf. 1 Co 15:28

*Cf. Ps 26:8

*Ps 84:2

*Cf. Jm 1:17

*Cf. Ep 4:14

*Cf. Ps 36:8

7. O charity, you stand at the right hand of the king, filling all things with your sweetness. You rule everything with your laws, you teach everything with your doctrine, you beautify everything with your glory. How sweet, how strong, how radiant, how glorious you are in that kingdom of your glory! In that kingdom of yours, you have imposed silence on all tongues, so that you alone may speak. You have annulled all laws and commandments, so that you alone are the eternal law, the new commandment, the new covenant. You have folded up all books, so that you alone hold the teacher's chair. You have taken away all prophets, so that you alone are to be questioned about the mysteries of God. You have destroyed all learning, so that for everything, you alone have the answer. Shutting your doors on faith and endurance and a great crowd of virtues with them, you send them to reign among us, while you tighten the bolts of your gates against them. You say: 'This kingdom belongs to the Lord* and his Christ. I am his handmaid, for ever ministering before him in this holy dwelling place.'*

*Ps 22:28

*Si 24:10

And so, O charity, our mother, o beauty and life of the virtues, all virtue draws from you the power to be truly virtue, from you it borrows garment and life. Certainly every virtue is naked without you, having no garment in which to clothe itself. Even if it has something, unless it is gilded by you, it is in no way a wedding garment. Further-more every virtue is not only deformed without you, having no charm or beauty, but since it lacks you, its form, it is obviously unformed and empty. If it does not draw its life from you, it is more than languid, it is lifeless. All virtues that are not quickened by you can have indeed the appearance of virtue but not the reality. On the contrary, lurking behind the shadow of an empty name, they are only the semblances of virtues, deceiving false worshippers with a false hope. It is you who have the right to say: 'Wisdom is mine, and sound judgment; discretion is mine, and *Pr 8:14* fortitude.'* In a word, all things are yours, *†Cf. 1 Co 3:23* for you are Christ's.† By the grace of our God, even we, in these lands so far away from your kingdom, fight under your command, since of God's mercy your command extends even this far. You are the true wisdom which reaches from end to *Ws 8:1* end mightily,* for you are the blessed end of all perfection; here the end of all justice, there the end of all glory.

8. What a difference exists between that brightness of yours that shines in every virtue like the noonday sun, and this brightness of yours by whose light we walk from the darkness of the shadow of death, gazing upon both. There your head is of *Cf. Gn 2:12* gold, and that gold the finest,* but here among us, are your feet, and we indeed are *Cf. Ps 110:1* your footstool.* Yet compared to your head, your feet are not so much golden as brazen. Under this form John saw the feet of the Son of man. 'His feet', he says, 'are *Rv 1:15* like bronze glowing in the furnace.'* How

different the vision of the head which the bride saw, and the vision of the feet which John saw! To the full extent that gold differs from bronze does that charity differ from this charity. That gold is precious and has a rich lustre, this gold is cheap and lacklustre. As it is written: 'the rear of its back is of pale gold.'* Yes, our charity is pallid from our various ills, whether from grief or heaviness or fear. Who could enumerate all the reasons for this pallor and all the forms of our ailments? Truly this is, as has been said, on the back of the dove, that is, of charity, and on the rear of its back, and it is of this that the vision is granted us in our present life. This is rather like Moses in days of old. After much earnest seeking after the face of God, he finally obtained with great difficulty the favor of seeing his back.* *Cf. Ex 33:23*

*Ps 68:13*

If you ask what is meant by the back of charity, and what by the rear of its back, let the apostle answer for me: 'Charity endures all things, believes all things, hopes all things, bears all things.'* Its back is *1 Co 13:7* suffering and endurance, the rear of its back is perseverence in suffering and the blessed end of perseverence.

Before this the psalm speaks of 'wings covered with silver,' to my mind an indication from the Holy Spirit that the wings are certainly golden within, but on the outside they are silvered. All the glory of charity is interior, and in comparison to that inner glory, all that glitters externally is as silver to gold.* This is why the golden *Cf. Ps 45:14* necklace promised to the bride by the companions of the spouse is studded with silver.* It is also not too far-fetched to regard the gold and silver wings as meaning that charity should be neither dumb nor deaf. It should ever immerse itself in the words of the Lord, tested by fire, and without ceasing it should speak or hear whatever serves to increase the kingdom of charity. So, brothers, if we also sleep between the two lots* of this twofold charity—namely, the charity in heaven and the charity here on earth—and if we make one a ladder to the other and likewise descend from one to the other,* then the wings of charity will grow upon us, golden within and silvered without. Yet it will also be granted us to bear our tribulations gladly, so that charity itself is not weakened too often by our various ills. It was surely for this reason that the feet of the Son of man appeared like bronze in a burning furnace, because it is always necessary to be purified in the fire of tribulation.* Yet even the charity which is in heaven, even that has its furnace, but there the intensity of the heat is the intensity of the bliss.

9. Let us round off what the bride's praise by a short and easy summary. Her spouse is Christ who has been made by God our justice and sanctification.* In consequence the love which is the summit and soul of the charity of his church, love due to God, includes that noblest form of charity which is in the heavenly Jerusalem. It shows us next that what is imperfect

in this charity resides in his holy ones here
on earth, as it were, in feet like to bronze.
To him be honor and glory, together
with the Father and the Holy Spirit,
one God, for ever and ever.
Amen.

## SERMON THIRTEEN

*The beginning of the thirteenth sermon.*
Of the charity with which God has loved the church: how it surpasses the charity with which he himself is loved by the church, first in the dignity of the one who loves, who is God, then in the spontaneous truth of the love, then in the very great age of the love, and lastly, in the strength and effect of the loving.

'HIS HEAD is of finest gold.'* For some days now, my brothers, we have been eagerly intent, not without the sweat of our brow, in tracking down this 'finest gold'. We have agreed with the advice of Solomon that we should seek after wisdom like wealth and dig it up like treasure.* But God is faithful.† Through his bounty we have to some degree found what we were seeking and there has been opened out to us a vein of finest gold, at least, of purest love. This is the kind of love the bride has for her spouse in that blessed country where everyone lives in joy, because they live in total love. Yet this gold, although in every way the finest, is still only the finest of its own kind. I am myself aware of a vein of gold richer than this, compared to which this can hardly

*\*Sg 5:11*

*\*Cf. Pr 2:4*
*†Cf. 1 Th 5:24*

231

even call itself gold! But what am I to do?
The vein is very deep and I have no spade
to dig with, and even if I had, I know I am
too weak to undertake such work. I know
what I will do!* I will ask the lord of
this treasure to send laborers† to dig with
me, and whatever gold we are able to dig
up we will carry into his treasury, after
repaying our debts and the cost of our
food. So, gracious Father, bless your servant
and say: 'Go ahead and prosper!'

2. It is incontrovertibly true that the
charity of God, with which he has loved his
church and goes on loving her, when compared with the charity with which he in
turn is loved by his church, is much more
precious, much more weighty, much more
solid, and much more brightly shining. It
is also incomparably prior and beyond all
reckoning purer. It is first in dignity, but
also first in origin and in eternity. First in
dignity, because the one who loves is the
creator, and what is loved is the created.
Prior in time, because by determining
beforehand what he would love, he made it
ready within himself so that it could love
him back in its turn. Prior in eternity,
because he so loved from eternity that he
predestined when he had loved from eternity, and that very eternity of loving is the
reason of the predestination. 'For those
whom he foreknew,' says the apostle, 'he
predestined to be made conformable to the
image of his Son.'* He 'foreknew,' it says,
as if he loved from the beginning, before all
ages. In the same way it is also said: 'for

*Lk 16:4*
*†Cf. Mt 20:4*

*Rm 8:29*

the Lord knows the way of the just.'*     *Ps 1:6*
This is the first and foremost reason why
we were called, why we were justified,
why we were glorified,* and of this it is     *Rm 8:30*
said: 'He saved me because he chose me.'*     *Ps 18:19*

O charity, in all truth astonishing and
pre-eminent, which has taken possession
of a heart of such great majesty, which
has filled him to overflowing with such
great tenderness, which has been intrinsic
in the eternal God from all eternity! It is
exceedingly lofty, extravagantly rich, wonderfully patient! From above comes the
dignity of its majesty, from within the
greatness of its sweetness, and in front
stretches the everlastingness of its duration.
For all ages then that charity contains
within itself all the reasons for our being
called, all the means of our being justified,
all the differences and measures of our
being glorified.* In the womb of his eternal     *Rm 8:30*
mercy, the charity of God has placed his
elect in a certain order and arrangement,
and when they are called, it is in that same
order that they immediately spring forth.
Likewise, by the same paths and at the same
pace as was there fixed for them, those
who are to be justified march forward, and
in the same measure and portion as fell to
each by lot, the glorified enter upon their
land of promise. So this eternal love keeps
a strong guard over the sons it has generated
in heaven. It holds them tight to its heart in
an indissoluble embrace, so that no one can
bring any charge against God's elect.* For     *Rm 8:33*
if it is God who begets, who calls, who

*Rm 8:34
justifies, who can condemn?*

3. Perhaps someone feels anxious about sin, that it may call him to account before our heavenly Father and break this covenant of love? In reply comes the voice of a real father, bursting out from the deepest vein of love: 'Whoever is born of God

*1 Jn 5:18
does not sin,* his origin in heaven protects him.' From the abundance of the heart the

*Mt 12:34
mouth* has spoken, but it is the heart of God, not man. In the human heart could never rise such great tenderness as to forgive the sinful son and attach no blame to him, whatever his sin. However blessed the generation of those sons, the greatest blessing is to have a Father so immeasurably ready to be merciful, so overflowing with compassion! Even if the sons in their folly deny their Father, heedless of the judgements of God, it is clear (as he himself bears witness) that he cannot forget the sons of his womb and cannot deny him-

*Cf. Is 49:15
self.* In short, from all eternity the charity of God has been our mother, and while knowing beforehand that we were going to sin against it, even then it was thinking deep within itself thoughts of peace and

*Jr 29:11
not of affliction.* It was pondering mercy, not judgement, and what kind of reconciliation would make it possible for us to come back again to grace. This is something that deserves all our wonderment, yet far outstrips all our capacity for wonder. Right from the beginning that love saw the sins we would commit against it, against a love so great and majestic: their

number, their greatness, their nature, and it
did not only hold us blameless for the
disloyalty of such grave evil, but even set
itself, with tenderest compassion, to see
how it could blot it out of its sight and
wipe it all away. O the power of charity!
O the great wonder of it in the Son who is
God of God! Even then his love saw that it
would be held in contempt by us con-
temptible little worms, yet of this contempt it took no notice at all. It was
anxious only to heal our wounds. It turned
its whole thought to what it could use as
medicine, to what was strongest in its
power, most healthful in its wisdom, sweetest in its goodness. Indeed, he repressed all
his wrath and compressed it into his mercy,
wholly pouring out his compassion upon
us all. He took counsel with his wisdom
about the most healing ointments and
about giving suck to his little ones, holding
them in his arms and giving them affec-
tionate kisses. He was for ever saying: 'What
can I do for my sons and daughters? They
have a place deep within me, no one can
take them from my heart, neither satan,
nor sin, nor death.* I have sworn to you, *Cf. Rm 8:35,38
my holy one, that this is my covenant
with them, that I will not be angry with
them for ever. Therefore, gird your sword
upon your thigh, o mighty one!* Charity *Ps 45:3
urges you forward, and all these are yours
for I bestow them on you. You are my
arm, on you I rely for help. In you the
work of saving them will be accomplished
with power and fidelity.'

*Mk 8:2

*Rm 1:4

*Cf. Is 53:5

In his turn, from within the bosom of the Father's tenderness, the Only-begotten Son made answer: 'My Father, may it be as you desire. I, too, have pity on this multitude,* and I go to blot out all their sins with your charity and my blood. So in the spacious womb of that eternal predestination Christ Jesus was predestined Son of God in power,* on whom the Father laid the sins of us all and on whom, as it is written, was laid the punishment of our peace.* Thereupon the Only-begotten Son of the Father did penance before the Father for our transgressions. He held up to the Father's gaze the evidence of his hands and feet and the blood of his sacred wounds. He interceded for us with his Father as a suppliant, and he took the greatest care to set before the Father's judgement seat the cause of our reconciliation. This is why the voices of the prophets speak of what will happen in the distant future as though it were far in the past. They are imitating that eternal wisdom who accomplished what was in the future, or rather, for whom there is no future and no past, but for whom everything is now and always present beneath the changeless gaze of eternity.

4. It is clear from the above how marvellous and various is the love with which God loves his church, and that this love comes before the love with which the church loves the Lord her God. It is higher in dignity, it is more intimate in sweetness, it is anterior in eternity. How will the one

love be able to encounter the other, which comes up from such a distance, which flows out of such an intimacy, and which hastens so impetuously and swiftly from times so far remote? 'Behold,' says the Lord, 'I came to meet them like a river of peace, like an overflowing torrent of glory.'* The love of God is indeed a river of peace, streaming out in its greatness and flowing in with gentle waters. At the same time it is a torrent, rushing along with mighty force and sweeping everything away with it. How, then, can the dove of God, the charity the church bears to him, make an adequate response when compared with this charity? The dove can only stand with drooping wing, now looking up to wonder at the majesty of this love, now gazing within to marvel at its goodness, and now looking back in amazement at its antiquity. If it summons all that is within it to bless, if it rouses all its bones to marvel, how, I ask you, can it have any more spirit in it, how can it open its mouth in any other way except to say in ecstacy of mind: 'Lord, who is like you* and what love is like yours?'

Alongside God's sublime love, the love of the church seems commonplace, straightened alongside its immensity, new and belated alongside its ageless eternity. What about purity? What if we were to make a comparison here? More than anything else, the charity of God is preeminent for its incomparable purity. It is not purged by fire or by other means; in

*Cf. Is 66:12

*Ex 15:12

*Ws 7:25

fact, nothing defiled can gain entrance to
it.* Rather, through the force of the
immensity of its own natural purity, it has
the power to purge away all that is impure.
That it is free and spontaneous greatly en-
hances the charm of this purity, and just
as it flows out in abundance from the rich
plenty of its own heart, so too it flows out
freely. It does not look for repayment but
rather lavishes itself in love, even with force
and insistence.

The treasure of our love is hidden in the
field of our heart and lies buried down in
the very depths. Only after great labor and
heavy sweat, only after giving up everything that we possess, are we finally able—
with difficulty—to dig up a little of it, and
the small amount eventually dug up is
found to be thoroughly impure and earthy.
To be of much use it must of necessity
first be smelted down in a great fire. For
this purification the fire of God's everlasting love is absolutely necessary. We must
beg from the Father of lights some little
spark from that great conflagration that
consumes everything in heaven, and then
we must lay sticks on it and, lying flat on
the ground, we must blow hard and do our
utmost with sighs and longings. We must
rouse it up in ourselves, until at last a
steady flame rises up from this little fire.
We shall never lack a good supply of sticks,
since we have at hand the huge and infinite forest of God's benefits, created from
all eternity and increasing every day into
infinity. Who can recount, who has the

power in some way to plumb with his
mind, all the mercies which the Lord has
prepared and lavished and displayed openly
both in his own self and in us?* If only we     *Cf. Si 18:4*
would every day make for ourselves a pile
of these sticks and put it on this fire! Then
indeed, all the trees of the wood will shout
for joy,* when they are handed over to this     *Ps 96:11*
most blessed fire. At the moment, their
branches and twigs seem glued to them,
and they grow without fruit, all because
they are not solemnly set aside for this
kind of purpose.

As we have said, then, the charity of God
has by its own nature the greatest purity.
Not only has it nothing that is impure, but
it has everything that is perfect in purity.
It has no need at all of kindness from
another, but rather lavishes abroad its own
kindness. Secure in its integrity, it does not
wait to be forestalled, but with spontaneous
generosity takes by surprise all who love
it, as yet far away by their actions.

All this has been said to show what God's
love is like, at least with respect to its predestination from eternity.

5. But the charity of God has more to
it than sweet and loving premeditations. It
is also powerful, and displays its strength in
activity. It is well worthwhile to probe
into its workings, to see its power, what
value it has, what weight, what brightness,
what solidity. Sometimes it is necessary for
a reality of such deep deliberation and long-
lasting silence to break into the open, and
a mystery so purposely concealed will find

it fitting to answer itself in a style in keeping with its magnificence. Following this
principle, the Lord Jesus, when lived among
us, for a long time did not walk about in
full view. For roughly thirty years he purposely kept himself to himself; his face was
*Is 53:3       as it were hidden and despised,* and in the
*Ps 18:11      meanwhile he made darkness his covering.*
But afterwards, in keeping with the words
of Isaiah, he came 'like a rushing stream,
which the spirit of the Lords drives for-
*Is 59:19      ward.'* He broke the long-standing silence
by opening his mouth and distilling the
honey of his lips, and he also broke for
ever his peaceful retreat by opening his
hands and displaying the power of his marvellous deeds. As the apostle says, at the
time of his good pleasure, the charity of
God came to reveal to his church the
mystery silent from immemorial ages and
*Cf. Rm 16:25  hidden in God alone.* He came out of his
marriage chamber to preach upon the
housetops what had been whispered in the
*Mt 10:27      privacy of the inner room.* Those eternal
ages were for our God like a time of contemplation and rest, indeed, like a sabbath.
Then the day came, in his own time, for
him to come out into the open and for
contemplation to display itself in action.
What had been for so long in labor at last
came forth. Let the womb of that eternal
love be opened, and let it bring forth for
*Cf. Is 45:8   us a savior.* Let it pour forth with him and
after him the whole race of the chosen,
conceived so long ago. This is in all reality
exactly what has happened. We have his

own words: 'I have kept silence, I have restrained myself. I will cry out like a woman in child-birth.'* And again: 'Shall I who bring others to birth, be sterile?' says the Lord God.* 'As the earth brings forth its shoots, and as a garden causes what is sown in it to spring up, so the Lord God will cause righteousness and praise to spring up before all the nations.'* So the Wisdom of God has come, raising his voice in our streets,* preaching to the world the charity of God. This is what he cries aloud: 'God so loved the world as to give his Only-begotten Son.'*

6. Listen, o church of God, listen and incline your ear!* To you the words are spoken, and to you alone have been given ears that can hear. Listen, I repeat; consider the great majesty of him who has loved you, how he has loved you from all ages, how undeserved this love has been, how great it is. You are bound to respond to this love with all your strength. Be careful how you make response! The one who loves you is exceedingly great, and you, utterly unworthy of being loved, are quite incapable of returning a love commensurate with so high an honor. Yet render what little you have, render completely all you can do and all you are, and that will content him. He does not seek your love so as to be enriched by you. Indeed, compared to his love, yours is a drop in a bucket! Even if it were perhaps a river, it still holds that 'all the rivers flow into the sea, and the sea is not made greater!'* But

*Is 42:14

*Is 66:9

*Is 61:11

*Pr 1:20

*Jn 3:16

*Cf. Ps 45:10

*Cf. Qo 1:7

you are yourself made very much greater!
Whenever you pour back into his fulness
whatever little love you have, in exchange
for your small amount you appropriate all
that fulness to yourself and you become
established upon all the blessings of your
Lord.

To attain to the eternity of this love is
far beyond your capacity. Then at least
ponder those eternal years in the desire of
your heart. Have everlastingly in mind the

*Cf. Ps 76:6 everlasting years of that everlasting love,*
because it abounds for you from everlast-
ing ages. Give thanks endlessly and always,
for you have so long beforehand been
anticipated by so great a majesty that
not even by putting to it all your mind
could you attain it even in the slightest.
God has loved you from all eternity: love
him, then, now, and forever! In him there
was no beginning to love, for you there
must be no ending. Even so, your response
cannot equal his. Just as he has no beginning to his love, just so he knows no end.
To this unsolicited love it is not enough to
make your own unsolicited gift, as if now
there were an equal interchange, with both
sides balanced. On your side is not a free
gift, but the payment of the debt you owe.
Yet this very circumstance is not the least
part of his infinite graciousness and un-
forced love, in that all the debt you pay he
takes as a kindness, receiving it as if it
really were a free gift.

Listen to how greatly you are loved:
'God so loved the world as to give his

Only-begotten Son.'* How strongly this
incites us to love! On this errand God has
sent the one and only Son of his love,
consubstantial with himself, to reveal his
love towards us and incline us to accept it.
O how sweet a messenger, and how very
sweet his message! He is the bearer of a
deep mystery and the angel of great counsel! Go forth to meet him, all you who feel
within yourselves the stirring of holy love!
Run to embrace him! Hasten to kiss him!
Bless in your heart the blessed one who
comes in the name of the Lord,* and bless
him who sent him! For from the goodness
of his heart and the depths of his love, the
Father has uttered a good Word,* and the
most certain proof of his great love is the
sending forth of his only-begotten Son. But
why did he send him, do you think? He
sent him in order to give, he gave him in
order to give himself and all that is his with
him. He gave him in order to deliver him
up for us, and on our behalf he did not
spare his only Son.*

God's beloved, look more closely still at
this love—its value, its weight, as said above,
its solidity and brightness. In every single
one of these qualities, compare your love
with his. You have, of course, shown the
value of your love in that you despised
everything, and even your own soul, so as
to acquire it for yourself. But this is the
value of God's love: he left the heavens and
all his friends and neighbors, who are
not here below, and he came down to you,
and he came to make you like himself, to

*Jn 3:16

*Mt 21:9

*Cf. Ps 45:1

*Cf. Jn 3:16

seek you and to take up his abode with you.

7. Let us see how earthly things compare with heavenly. Hear now: to assert more firmly the truth of his love, the Son left his Father and the Father his Son. Of the Son, it has been truly said: 'A man will leave father and mother and cleave to his wife.'* Of the Father and to the Father, we have the cry of the Son: 'Why have you deserted me?'* It was indeed a great cry that the Lord Jesus uttered at that time and place. That cry was the thunderpeal of infinite charity and unspeakable tenderness, so intent on recommending to us the Father's love that for our sake he showed himself forsaken and deserted. I do not see how the value of that charity could ever be more highly recommended than when it was made so clear, by the Father as well as the Son, how much it cost them. Both of them paid the price of dereliction since, as we have said, each deserted the other, the Father his Son, and the Son his Father.

Let us see, then, what has been purchased at this high price. 'You have been bought', says the apostle, 'at a great price.'* What are you, o man, to have been valued so highly and esteemed of such exceptional worth? Certainly, if you compare yourself to what you are, what is more shameful; but compared to what you cost, what is more precious? O wonderful exchange,* and a wonderful motive for the exchange! That majesty whom the heaven of heavens cannot contain endured being

*Gn 2:24

*Ps 22:1

*1 Co 6:20

*o admirabile commercium— antiphon from Vespers of the Circumcision.

bought and sold at the cheapest price. On the other hand, that most abject thing, man, was purchased by God, and so there was an exchange of grandeur. Because of the inestimable value put upon him, he in became himself inestimable. From this day forth at least, o man, be ashamed to be compared to the brute beasts, when you have been bought at such a price! Try even now to understand the honor once rendered you, and its heavy cost! Hold it to your heart with every reverence! Give a return of love to your purchaser, and glorify him for your price. Do not ever again give your honor to strangers and your years to the merciless.*    *Pr 5:9

8. To make quite sure of the weight of this charity, let us weigh it, weight for weight; the weight of divine love against the weight of human sinfulness. Heavy indeed, beyond bearing, like the sands of the sea, is the infinite mass of sinfulness. Man cannot reckon it. Yet this excessive load of huge stones is hanging round humanity's neck and dragging it down beneath the mighty waters.* The charity of    *Cf. Ex 15:20 God runs to meet his church, now on the very point of sinking under, and in his hand he bears the scales of justice. And so the church with all its sinfulness is weighed in one pan, and on the other, directly opposite, the charity of God lays itself to be weighed, having with it the God-man, his cross and his blood, and a very large bundle of myrrh, carefully gathered from the sufferings of Christ.* (Afterwards, the    *Cf. Sg 1:13

bride placed this between her breasts as a bundle of lightest weight, but in that pan it was found very heavy indeed.) In the presence of charity, all sinfulness disappeared in an instant like a cloud, and it showed on the scales as weighing nothing at all.* Because of its excessive weight, charity, together with the God-man, dipped right down to the depths, to where the church had been on the verge of going, and the church, through the power of the scale where she swings, rose up on high, to where Christ had been about to go.

*Cf. Is 40:15

9. You are truly just and merciful, o Lord. Your right hand is filled with justice,* and your mercy is full of discernment. In the work of your salvation there is no dispute at all between your mercy and your truth, for, just as always, you act on your Father's behalf so that they may come together in a kiss of peace. With very great love, then, God has taken thought for the church, has redeemed it at the price of charity, has lifted it up to heaven. Why then should he not bind it to himself for ever with indissoluble and firmest love? Beneath her head she has for softest pillow the left hand of her spouse,* the everlasting memorial of all he has endured on her account. Embracing her, she has his right hand in all its holiness,* the eternal reminder of all the blessings he has shown her, especially in admitting her to the full fruition of the sweetness of union with him. Hence, the firmness of divine love binds closely together this holy

*Ps 48:10

*Cf. Sg 2:6

*Cf. Sg 2:6

covenant, and is itself the everlasting sweetness of the bond.

10. Furthermore, who can describe,
who can even gaze at, with sufficient
wonder, the brightness of that glowing
charity? It moves always from brightness
into brightness, and with love to strengthen
and comfort the eyes, light in seen in light.*    *Cf. 2 Co 3:18*
The charity of the church, with which it
loves God, is surely also itself a light and a
fire strongly flaming, but all this power to
burn and shine it draws from that other
charity. Eternally it draws from it what
eternally it pours back into it, and so its
charity will never grow dim or faint. It
sees in its own self, and the sight never
wearies it, how great is God's love, how
ancient, how sublime, how generous, how
spontaneous, how precious, how weighty,
how firm, how radiant with light. It will
see in that day how well the bride did to
say: 'the head of my spouse is the finest
gold,'* and Paul to say: 'the head of Christ    *Sg 5:11*
is God,'* and John to say: 'God is love.'†    *1 Co 11:3*
And now, you who are the font of this    †1 Jn 4:8
love, the Father of our Lord Jesus Christ,
bless us gloriously with that love through
the only Son of your love,
who with you lives and
reigns, God, for ever
and ever.
Amen.

## SERMON FOURTEEN

*The beginning of the fourteenth sermon.*
Why the love which is God, in which the
whole Trinity goes out wholly to itself in
love, is incomparably higher than the twofold charity which was discussed previously.
Why the strength of charity in its very origin
is so great that three are completely one, in
power, wisdom, goodness and simplicity
of essence.

A T THE COMMAND OF CHARITY,
my brothers, I have set my shoulder
to the task of searching out the
threefold vein of charity. For my part, I
am drenched with perspiration, and yet
whatever has been achieved, however small,
charity itself has achieved it. To the extent,
then, that love has made it possible, three
sermons have investigated the love of the
church of God, and of God for his church.
We have seen the love of the church in the
time of its probation here below and in the
day of its power in heaven above. We have
seen, too, the love God had within himself
from the beginning, a love of pre-election,
and how that love afterwards showed
itself in action. But with respect to this
new commandment, the work is so very
laborious that I confess I hesitate as to

what I need to do. The promptings of love itself—if it really is his voice and not another that sounds like it—urges me to speak a little of that noblest love, that of the Father for his only-begotten Son. It urges me to make at least some stammering attempt. My great fear is that charity itself may cause me to be regarded as an intruder, though I shall bear quite cheerfully being judged something of a fool! However, I am going to follow the hand that draws me and the goad that spurs me forward, but on this condition: not even for one moment must charity let go of the hand of the poor servant that follows it. It is an arduous climb up the slopes of this sublime mountain, where there is many and many a stone to be stumbled on, and among the stones it is easy to slip and have a hard fall.

To begin our journey at the foot of the mountain, we recognize that two commandments of charity have flowed out to us from the eternal fountain of charity: love of God and of our neighbor. These are the twofold means of salvation which our king and our God, who ordained salvation for Jacob,* ordained for us from heaven, by the hand of our savior. In these is the essential meaning of all the words of the Lord God, and a short and easy summary of all his laws. They are very well worth knowing, for on those two tablets the finger of God himself has written about his very own love. He has, as it were, shaped and chiselled them out of Mount Sinai with us in mind.* That mountain

*Cf. Ps 44:4

*Cf. Ex 31:18

is in a real sense the mount of charity, a
rich and fertile mountain, in which God
takes delight to dwell.* He has dwelt there
from the beginning and he will dwell
there for ever.

  *Ps 68:16

With those laws it is impossible to find
fault, to claim they are too long-winded or
too new-fangled or too irksome. They are a
summary, so they are short; they are
eternal, so they are old; they are loving, so
they are easy. They are in fact so eternal
that their author, the ancient of days, himself lives by these same laws, and has done
so from the beginning. 'I know', says
Jesus, 'that the command of my Father
is life everlasting.'* If charity is life everlasting, and it truly is this, then he who
lives eternally, lives by charity, because he
is charity. So their noble origin makes those
laws not only easy but very lovable. It is
from the love of God that they originate,
and to see such great majesty living by
them, as we have said before, renders them
most lovely and compelling.

  *Jn 12:50

  2. The greatest commandment goes like
this: 'You shall love the Lord your God
with all your heart and with all your soul
and with all your strength and with all your
mind.'* And the second is very similar:
'You shall love your neighbor as yourself.'*
These two commandments God has prac-
tised from the beginning, for it was by
these same laws and standards of charity
that he loves his only-begotten Son. He has
not neglected one jot or tittle of them. On
the contrary, he has wholly observed the

  *Mk 12:30
  *Mt 22:39

law in all its wholeness, and he has fulfilled it without any omission or interruption. The only Son of the Father, too, from the beginning of the days of his eternity, agreed to these same laws with all his soul and all his strength. We would do wrong to take these words as insufficiently salted, because they have been served up to us carefully seasoned with exactly the same salt. When we sit down to table, our mother wisdom goes to the greatest trouble to flavor what she gives us with just the amount of seasoning that will make it palatable to her little ones. For just as if she were to contract her mouth to the narrow limits of ours by stammering, so by reshaping our mouths to the lines of her own, she is able in the end to bring forth for herself perfect praise from the mouth *Mt 21:16* of babes and sucklings.* You often hear the Father saying of his Son: 'My heart has *Ps 45:1* uttered a good word,'* and when he finds *Cf. Ac 13:22* a man after his own heart,* it is without any doubt his only-begotten Son. He calls him also his beloved, of whom he says: *Mt 12:18* 'My soul is well pleased.'* And there are those words of the Father to the Son: *Ps 110:3* 'Before the daystar, I begot you.'*

3. The Father, who is the deepest source of charity and the purest channel of living water, therefore, loves God his Son with his whole heart, because with his whole reason, intelligence and wisdom. He loves him with his whole soul, because with his whole will, goodness and loving-kindness. He loves him with his whole

strength, because with his whole justice, power and resolution. He loves him with his whole mind, because with his whole memory and eternity and changelessness. But his neighbor, whom he loves as himself, is this very same Son, our neighbor too, neighbor to him through love and to us through compassion. By nature, he is a neighbor to both, and this is why he was made the mediator between the two. No one but he was so well fitted to the task of accomplishing this union, because he came already joined to each side.

So from the beginning the Father loved his Son with all his wisdom, and through this loving generation, he brought it about that the Son himself should be all his wisdom. He loved him with all his goodness, and in the same way he brought it about that he should also be all his goodness. He loved him too with all his strength and all his justice, and so established him as his holy right arm and the fulness of all his justice.* He loved him with all the endless awareness of his eternity, and so he truly brought it about that he should be his eternal and changeless only-begotten Son. In a word, he gave himself wholly to his Son, and loved him wholly with the whole of himself.

*Cf. Ps 98:1*

So the whole of the Only-begotten Son is in the whole of the Father, occupying the heart of his wisdom, filling the spirit of his goodness, overflowing the depths of his strength, satisfying the great womb of his eternity. He is in the Father's heart,

*Cf. Rm 11:33*

searching all the depths of his wisdom and knowledge.* He is in the Father's soul, exploring all his treasures of goodness and kindness. He is in the sanctuary of his justice, entering into all the abysses of judgement and the secret places of his verdicts. He is in his mind, the very same simple and changeless being, and because of this, he is the origin of all that is, holding it in the grasp of his truth.

*Sg 5:11*

*Cf. 1 Co 11:3; 1 Jn 4:8*

Last of all, if we maintain the bride's way of celebrating, then the reason why 'his head is the finest gold',* is that the head of Christ, as the apostle testifies, is certainly God, and God, as John testifies, is love.* In the truest sense, God is love, and the finest love, for he gives himself so wholly to the whole of his only Son that he reserves absolutely nothing to himself. There is nothing he possesses, nothing that he is, which he has not utterly handed over to his Son.

4. Let us pursue the comparison with gold, and with this charity also, let us examine its qualities. This charity is radiantly bright especially as regards wisdom, most precious as regards goodness, very weighty as regards power and justice, and lastly, immensely firm as regards its essential eternity.

*Ws 7:29*
†*Cf. Ws 7:26*

I do well to speak of wisdom as light, for, as the wise man says: 'compared to light, she is the purer',* since she has the very brightness of eternal light.† It is fitting, too, to speak of goodness as being precious, because there is nothing more valuable, nothing dearer. This is specially so for us, for it was goodness that showed itself in paying the price of our redemption. Weight seemed to me an appropriate description of strength and justice and for this reason, that weight can be twofold, upwards or downwards, and strength and justice render to every man according to his works;* *\*Cf. Mt 16:27* to the one, what is above, and to the other, what is below. With reason, too, firmness is applied to eternity, because it is changeless in its simplicity and exists in a massive internal harmony by the law of its own firm solidity. Therefore God, the head of the spouse, is the finest charity, because most full of wisdom, of loving-kindness, of justice and power, of everlasting changelessness.

The spouse is the only-begotten of the Father, and he is loved by the Father as unique, as coequal, as consubstantial. I take it that the evangelist is indicating these aspects of love when he tells us: 'In the beginning was the Word, and the Word was with God, and the Word was God.'* *\*Jn 1:1* When he says: 'In the beginning was the Word,' turn your mind to the unfathomable mystery of the love within God's heart. Think of its unimaginable sweetness, which no one knows, or can know, except only the Father. It was of this that the only-begotten spoke: 'No one knows the Son except the Father.'* *\*Mt 11:27* When the evangelist adds: 'The Word was with God', think of how the Son is in every way equal to the Father. It is the great sin of blasphemy to think or say that the Son is lower than the Father, and the man who for any reason ranks the Father of majesty higher than his only-begotten Son will be arraigned before him as a sinner. If there is any honor paid to the Father which in some way excludes his Son, then he rises to avenge it with his own hand, as if it were as much as insult to the Father as to the only-begotten. Finally, when the evangelist concludes: 'The Word was God', turn your thoughts to the Son as consubstantial with the Father. There is certainly but one God, as Moses proclaimed to Israel: 'Your God is one God,'* yet since the Word is God, he is just as truly God as is the Father. In receiving from the Father the essence of divinity, he receives also the power of having the same substance as he has himself. Here is clear proof of how unimaginably great is the overflowing love of the Father for the Son, and how sweet and strong is the passion of the font for its fountain of sweetness. The Father grants his Son to be in him as his most intimate self, as his uniquely beloved, as the Father's perfect likeness. He grants him to be before him as coequal in majesty, power and eternity.

*Dt 6:4

There is this, too. As the Father is the beginning with respect to his Son, so too the Son is the beginning with respect to the Holy Spirit, and just as the Holy Spirit proceeds from the Father, so likewise does he proceed from the Son. For the Holy Spirit is love itself, and he is a font of love springing

up from both Father and Son. This is why
he is said to be the love of the Father and
the Son, because he who is love proceeds
from both by their mutual will and their
equal love. So we see how admirable and
plenteous is the richness of love in the
blessed Trinity, and what a great river it is
of most sacred joy. From the fullness of
this joy the Father utters the whole of himself to the Son, and in the same way the
Son, together with the Father, utters the
whole of himself to the Holy Spirit, so that
these three are one single font of love. The
love of this unity will never slacken, for it
is a unity of love that there holds blissful
sway. There is, of course, nothing within
the indivisible unity of the most holy
Trinity which is not to be praised and
reverenced in the highest degree, but it is
no cause for wonder if charity has a place
of special privilege and power here at the
very source and font of its own being. God
has the power of making those who are
joined to God, one spirit with him.* In     *1 Co 6:17*
the strength and truth of this, then, is it to
be wondered at, if the Father and the Son
and the Holy Spirit, each one of whom is
charity, should together be but one charity,
the charity of a single essence, and the
essence of a single charity?

5. Even here below, so very distant
from that font, we see how love is everywhere working to maintain its preeminence,
how it struggles to rule as king, as befits its
race and kind, whether as good among the
good or as evil among the evil. Since it

naturally possesses the innate force of drawing those whom it seizes towards a strong
desire for unity, it draws with as much
strength as sweetness, and the sweeter it is,
the nearer to unity. Every human bond
serves the cause of love, whether in the
relationship of parents to children or children to parents, whether in that deeper and
closer relationship of a husband to his wife
and a wife to her husband, whether in any
one at all of the various relationships that
make up human society. In all of these,
love attracts them either to advance or to
strive to advance towards a simple principle
of unity. They follow the leadership of love,
to their good if it is a good love, to their
evil if it is evil. Nevertheless, each and every
kind of love reveals some small resemblance
to that true and everlasting love, if anyone
takes the trouble to look for it.

6. Not only in rational creatures, but
even in those who are moved by appetite
alone, we are perpetually being instructed
by examples all around us,* though they
lose their value through their very frequency. Yet the Wisdom of God played
before his Father's face over the whole
expanse of the earth,† and he plays also
before the face of those who learn how to
join in Wisdom's play by rejoicing and
feeling wonder. He presses upon our attention symbols and images of that high love,
and they are not unworthy of it.

To take an example which the Wisdom
of God used of himself, we see how the hen
yearns over her chickens, how tenderly and

*Pr 8:31.
*See Augustine,
Tractatus in
Ioannem
24.1; PL 35;
1595; CC 36:244
†Pr 8:31

how often she warms them against her
breast, how repeatedly she gives birth. The
keener her affection, the harsher her voice,
and in a wonderful fashion, she yearns with
affection towards her young in proportion
to her hoarseness. What are we to make of
the way she passes, as it were, wholly into
a state of love, and shows this not only by
rasping her voice, but by fluffing out her
feathers, by drooping her body, by an-
xiously running to and fro, by constant
service, by sleepless watch, by brooding
over her chicks with selfless devotion?* *\*Cf. Mt 23:37*
Do we not also find that sheep, the meekest
of animals, in dealing with their lambs put
forth the full force of their affection?
They bleat tenderly, they provide sweet
nourishment, they lead them about continually, they defend them vigorously. Soon
they mount horns, and they are armed with
these for the safety of the lambs, even at
the cost of their own death.

Perhaps you will call this kind of thing a
game, and of course you are quite right,
but it is a serious game. It is the Wisdom of
God who is playing and anyone who
watches the game must see to it that he
does not mock the player and hear: 'We
piped to you, and you did not dance.'* *\*Cf. Mt 11:17*
Let them rather play and dance and leap
before the ark of the Lord, with the
Wisdom of God the Father,* who from the *\*Cf. 2 S 6:16*
heights of his love uses the mirror of visible
creation to send some brilliant rays of light
down into our darkness. For there is no
creature, rational or irrational, that is

without a voice, none without a tongue. In the innate desires of their instinctive affections, all things speak to us of the ineffable mystery of eternal love, if only we take the trouble to notice. If we do not, then all these things are dumb to us and we are deaf to them.

7.   Leaving for the moment the question of irrational affection, the force of love binds together into one a pair of friends, partners in the same likes and dislikes.* Mothers feel such intense love for their sons that no matter how they pour it out, it can hardly show itself in its fullness; they seem almost to be wracking their bowels all over again with the vehemence of their affection. Then, there is that most beautiful of loves, the love of a husband and a wife, one even stronger than those already mentioned, for it so unites them both that they become two in one flesh.* Finally, we have that love, blessed beyond all others, the love that draws a rational soul even as far as union with its creator, so that he who is joined to God is one spirit with him.* In this context, then, I put the question: what will charity not be able to achieve in the very font from which it takes its origin?

At this point, who will wonder if the fountain of love, at the very source of its being, springs forth with greater force, leaps up more joyously, froths and foams with more abandon, tastes sweeter, is more crystalline in purity, and more vigorous in strength? How is the marvel of the charity

*Cf. Aelred, Spir amic I: PL 195: 665D, 667BC; CF 5:00.

*Mt 19:5

*1 Co 6:17

within the blessed Trinity clearly to be
distinguished from all the other virtues
which it effects throughout the rational
world, if not in this: that by its wonderful
and surpassing virtue, the essence of the
blessed Trinity is one, because everywhere,
those who love aright become one in heart
and soul?* In others, there is union; here, *Cf. Ac 4:32*
it is unity. In others, the effect takes place
as long as they love aright. Here, it is not a
question of effect, but of taking origin and
flowing out and streaming forth from each
one to each of the others, and from each of
the others to each one. The Son loves the
Father with a love absolutely equal to the
love with which he himself is loved by the
Father, meeting such and so great a Father
as befits such and so great a Son, with an
interchange of love in all respects the same.
So it is written of him: 'And his meeting is
at his highest point.'* In fact, to meet *Ps 19:6*
means to respond on even terms, as is likewise said of the Father by the Son: 'Rouse
yourself to meet me and see.'* Also the *Ps 59:4*
Holy Spirit, who is love proceeding from
both, hastens back with equal love to his
beginning, the Father and his only-begotten
Son, from whom he flows as a living and
never-failing font, and whom he embraces
with the total love that is himself.

8. Since charity is twofold in nature,
not only a feeling of well-wishing, but,
when possible, a doing of good deeds, it
delights that supreme and eternal charity
to make even the creature able to receive
him and to enter into a blessed partnership.

*Cf. Sg 1:2

But this is the glory of charity, to be lavish
to the needy because of its own fulness,
and to pour out from its richness on those
who are without, seeing that its name is
truly 'as oil poured out.'\* Hidden treasure
and secret charity: what use is there in
either? Since the love of these three for one
another is so superabundant, how could
each not glorify the other with all his
might? 'Father,' says the Son, 'glorify your
Son, so that your Son may glorify you.'\*
Of the Holy Spirit likewise, the Son says:
'He will glorify me'\* when he comes. If
we must be very careful to keep clearly in
view and make all our works tend to this
end, that in all we do God is to be
glorified, how much more does God himself, who alone knows how deserving he is
of every honor, owe befitting glory to
his holy name? He confirms this himself,
when he says over and over again in the
scriptures: 'I will do it on account of
myself' or 'on account of my name'\* or
'on account of my servant David',\* who
is Christ.

*Jn 17:1

*Jn 16:4

*Cf. Is 48:9
*Cf. Is 37:35

All the works of God have two ends in
view: to share his love with his creatures
and so make them blessedly happy; and
then, from his creatures' happiness, to
glorify his love. The sharing of love consists in lavishing gifts and in pouring out
compassion, and so, by a wonderful arrangement of God's wisest love, provision has
been made first for the free generosity of
his giving and then, almost by stealth, for
the entrance on the scene of wretchedness

in many guises. So there is ample room for his infinite pity, and where wretchedness abounded, pity abounded all the more.* *Cf. Rm 5:20 Thus the one man who saw reality perfectly referred everything, and taught us also to refer everything, to the glory of God. When he was asked about the cause of the blindness of the man born blind, he answered that it was to make manifest the works of God.* He attributed the reason *Cf. Jn 9:3 for the death of Lazarus to the same end.* *Cf. Jn 11:4 In the same way, Paul, dealing with those very deep questions as to why God has established all things in unbelief and why transgression has crept in and why scripture establishes all things under sin, gives a short, terse answer to them all. He sees all these reasons as interconnected, the full revealing of the mercy of God, the glorious shining forth of grace in its rich plenitude, the giving to believers of the promise of Jesus Christ.* *Cf. Rm 5:20

All that has been said makes it unmistakably clear that whether we speak of predestination of the saints or of the love of God for the saints, the beginning and the end is the love of the blessed Trinity giving its whole self to itself in love. It is certainly the beginning, for it is the perpetual cause, overflowing to them out of its own goodness. It is truly the end, for to its glory love itself and all the effects of love are blissfully directed. In this end, the blessed church of God's elect rests in the end that has no end, giving glory, in the wonderful and incomprehensible love of the blessed

Trinity, to its most joyful and indivisible unity, from whose gracious overflow the church herself becomes deserving of love, predestination, justification and glory.*

*\*Cf. Rm 8:30*

9. But now it is time for me to lay my finger to my lips and bow down to ask forgiveness for my folly and rashness. I am a man of unclean lips,* and what I have dared to touch on far exceeds my capacity and learning. It would indeed be a very great thing for me, I do not say to untie the latchet of the shoe of Christ,* but even to touch it. How much more, then, to hold in my unworthy grasp that head of his, of finest gold,* and the crown on his head? To take it upon myself to lift a weight so exceedingly heavy? But now, pardon my rashness, Lord Jesus. In my folly, your love urged me on, or at least, the longing for your love. Within the limits of what we are, Lord, bring it about by the decree of your mercy that discretion and love each find their right place, so that one does not go beyond its fitting end and the other attains its longed-for end, you who

*\*Is 6:5*

*\*Cf. Jn 1:27*

*\*Sg 5:11*

live and reign with God the Father
in the unity of the Holy Spirit,
God, for ever and ever.
Amen.

END OF VOLUME ONE

CUMULATIVE INDEX WILL FOLLOW
THE FINAL VOLUME

# ABBREVIATIONS

Asspt      Bernard of Clairvaux, *Sermo in assumptione B. V. M.*

CC      Corpus Christianorum series. Turnhout, Belgium.

CF      Cistercian Fathers Series.

Coll.      *Collectanea o.c.r.; Collectanea cisterciensia.*

Csi      Bernard of Clairvaux, *De consideratione ad Eugeniam tertiam libri quinque (Five Books on Consideration)*

DSp      *Dictionnaire de Spiritualité.* Paris, 1932–

Ep(p)      Letter(s)

OB      *Sancti Bernardi Opera,* edd. Jean Leclercq, H. M. Rochais, C. H. Talbot. Rome, 1957–

PL      J. P. Migne, *Patrologiae cursus completus, series latina.* 221 volumes. Paris, 1844–64.

RB      *Regula monachorum sancti Benedicti (St Benedict's Rule for Monks)*

Spir amic      Aelred of Rievaulx, *De spirituali amicitia (On Spiritual Friendship)*

N.B. Biblical names and citations have been made according to the nomenclature and enumeration of the Jerusalem Bible.

| | | | |
|---|---|---|---|
| Ac . . . Acts | | 1 K . . . 1 Kings | |
| Am . . . Amos | | 2 K . . . 2 Kings | |
| Ba . . . Baruch | | Lk . . . Luke | |
| 1 Ch . 1 Chronicles | | Lm . Lamentations | |
| 2 Ch . 2 Chronicles | | Lv . . . Leviticus | |
| 1 Co . 1 Corinthians | | Mk . . . Mark | |
| 2 Co . 2 Corinthians | | Ml . . . Malachi | |
| Col . . Colossians | | Mt . . Matthew | |
| Dn . . . Daniel | | Nb . . Numbers | |
| Dt . Deuteronomy | | 1 P . . . 1 Peter | |
| Ep . . Ephesians | | 2 P . . . 2 Peter | |
| Est . . . Esther | | Ph . . Philippians | |
| Ex . . . Exodus | | Pr . . Proverbs | |
| Ezk . . . Ezekiel | | Ps . . . Psalms | |
| Ga . . Galatians | | Qo . Ecclesiastes | |
| Gn . . Genesis | | Rm . . Romans | |
| Hab . . Habakkuk | | Rv . . Revelation | |
| Heb . . Hebrews | | 1 S . . 1 Samuel | |
| Ho . . . Hosea | | 2 S . . 2 Samuel | |
| Is . . . Isaiah | | Sg . . Song of Songs | |
| Jb . . . . Job | | Si . . Ecclesiasticus | |
| Jg . . . Judges | | Tb . . . . Tobit | |
| Jl . . . . Joel | | 1 Th 1 Thessalonians | |
| Jm . . . James | | 2 Th 2 Thessalonians | |
| Jn . . . . John | | 1 Tm . . 1 Timothy | |
| 1 Jn . . . 1 John | | 2 Tm . . 2 Timothy | |
| 2 Jn . . . 2 John | | Tt . . . . Titus | |
| 3 Jn . . . 3 John | | Ws . . . Wisdom | |
| Jr . . . Jeremiah | | Zc . . Zechariah | |
| Jude . . . 1 Jude | | | |